OWN YOUR STORY BEFORE
YOUR STORY OWNS YOU

Albert Schmick

Eph 3:16

God bless!

Own Your Story

BEFORE YOUR STORY OWNS YOU

ALBERT SCHUESSLER

Name and Claim Your Valuable Story

XULON PRESS

Xulon Press
2301 Lucien Way #415
Maitland, FL 32751
407.339.4217
www.xulonpress.com

Paperback ISBN-13: 978-1-6628-4833-9
Ebook ISBN-13: 978-1-6628-4834-6

This book is dedicated to my grandson Rodney Cole Schuessler.

Rodney was born with hydrocephalus on March 13, 1984. He passed away and was ushered into the arms of Jesus on June 23, 1987. It was through his life and death that I began my journey in owning my story. I will always cherish my memories of Rodney as he struggled and won the battle.

Abba, Abba little boy. You are my hero.

Endorsements

Albert Schuessler is a walking sermon of the truths in this book. Over thirty-five years ago, Albert spent two entire days sharing, one on one, this story with me. My life and ministry were changed forever. Instead of me centered or church centered, I became Christ centered!

Pastor Jim Burns, Liberty Baptist church, Van Wert, Ohio

Pastor Al is the real deal—he has experienced what he is writing about. As Al communicates how to move forward from brokenness, he is refreshingly authentic and transparent as he shares his story about struggles he has faced. Al teaches us through his story that change is possible by understanding who we are in Christ. Pastor Al's teaching is incredibly practical, encouraging, and helpful, and will be beneficial to you as the next chapter of the story of your life is written.

Pastor Dean Hughes, Eastside Baptist Church, Topeka, Kansas

I enjoy Pastor Al Schuessler's down-to-earth and easy to understand wisdom in *Own Your Story Before Your Story Owns You*. I can relate to being a "broken crayon," and loved, being reminded that God still uses "broken crayons" to color His story. Pastor Schuessler reminds us that God has a part for all of us "broken crayons." God desires to use our stories for His beautiful picture on this earth. May you be encouraged and challenged to use your life story to show the world the love of our amazing God!

Pastor Jeff Isaacs, Riverlawn Christian Church, Wichita, Kansas

Contents

Foreword

I am honored to be writing the foreword to *Own Your Story Before your Story Owns You* by Pastor Al Schuessler. Pastor Schuessler is not only my associate pastor, but my friend and mentor of many things. In this book, you will find he understands that one of the largest obstacles people must get through is to be comfortable with their past. He explores the shame and dishonor people feel when they think they are the only one who has made any mistakes. Pastor Schuessler gives guidance to those that are hurting and think their past cannot be forgiven. He helps them understand that Jesus loves broken people and wants to help put them back together to make them whole again. The one thing that resonates with me throughout *Own Your Story Before Your Story Owns You* is that you have to own your story, however it may look, before it owns you where you are right now. As John Maxwell was quoted as saying, "It does not matter if you fall down as long as you pick-up something from the floor while you get up." I pray this book helps you transform your life.

God Bless,

Pastor Bruce Thomas

Preface

I believe that everyone's story is important. I have come to realize after many years of pastoring that we often have a fear of sharing our stories with other people. My interest in writing a book about accepting and owning your story materialized as I was struggling with my own life story. In my mid-forties, I concluded that I had to own my story. I had placed my story in the lock box of my soul and threw the key away. I then had the tendency to hide my story behind Christianity. I would only express a small portion of my life, only the good things I wanted others to see. For some reason my story became what I called a fake story. My conduct was not in alignment with the Word of God at times. In reality, instead of *owning my story, my story owned me.*

As I looked back on my experiences I saw that I had traveled down a certain path that brought me to the juncture of owning my story. Owning my story began to eliminate the fear I had been experiencing about my story. The ownership of my story eventually opened my story wide open to the extent that it exposed my true identity. It was at this point that I came to accept the fact that I am okay with *living within my own skin.* I no longer tried being someone else, living in their skin, because I thought they were better than me. I no longer needed their identity but was satisfied with my own identity.

I want to share that journey with you for you to be free to open and share your story, as well. For you to come to the place that you are okay with *living within your own skin.* I like to call the process "name and claim your valuable story." My parents gave me a name when I was born, that is who I am, and that is my story. Thus, the title of the book is *Own Your Story Before Your Story Owns You.*

As you read the pages of this book, my challenge is for you to be able to accept who you are and "name and claim your valuable story" and "own your story" as your journey carries you on into the future. Hey, it's your fingerprint on your birth certificate and it's your DNA, so why not just go ahead right now and claim your valuable story.

Acknowledgments

To my wife

A special thank you to my wife Shirley who encourages me to fulfill my dreams in writing. She is my greatest cheerleader in everything that I do and accomplish. She gives me the space needed to be alone and to pen my thoughts upon paper. Thank you for the sacrifice you make while I pursue this segment of my journey in life.

To my friend

Thanks to Javier Jimenez for the time and effort you have invested in taking pictures of me for this book I have written. You are a creative photographer, knowing the exact backgrounds and poses for each occasion. I appreciate your willingness to take time to find the best picture setting for this very special project.

To my church

Thank you to Glenville Church, Wichita, Kansas, and its pastor Bruce and Lesley Thomas. While being on staff well into my senior years of life, you have given me the opportunity to keep my mind fresh and creative. Along with my family, Glenville Church motivates me to press toward the mark of the high calling of God.

Introduction

"Let your story bring glory to God's glory"
—Albert Schuessler

For all our days are passed away in thy wrath: we spend our years as a tale that is told. The days of our years are threescore years and ten; and if by reason of strength they be fourscore years, yet is their strength labor and sorrow; for it is soon cut off, and we fly away. Who knoweth the power of thine anger? even according to thy fear, so is thy wrath. So, teach us to number our days, that we may apply our hearts unto wisdom.

—Psalm 90:9–12 KJV

It is almost unbelievable to think about the first life that was breathed into the first human being. His name was Adam, and he became a living soul. Human life must exist and live in order to write a human story. This event took place in the book of Genesis. *"Then the Lord God formed the man from the dust of the ground. He breathed the breath of life into the man's nostrils, and the man became a living person"* (Gen. 2:7 NLT). Genesis means origin, beginning, or in other words, the very first to exist. It was at this point Adam became the first storyteller in the universe.

I think it would be exciting to own the first story ever told. I suppose it would be exciting until your whole story is shared throughout the entire world as if it were cast upon a giant movie screen for everyone to see and make judgment about, good, or bad.

I'm sure there are certain behaviors that Adam would have liked to have swept under the shag carpet in the Garden of Eden. The scripture says in Genesis 3:10 that Adam heard the voice of God and hid from God. On the other hand, there would be certain accomplishments that would make him look good and cause him to say, "Look at me and see how great I am." I'm sure it was easy for pride to fester in his mind, and he would no doubt brag about the fact that he was the first one that received form and life and became the first storyteller. So, the saga of human storytelling began a long time ago and has continued down through the ages even until today.

At present you will find the focus on your story, which is as important and exciting as the first story ever told. Your story is one among countless numbers of stories that have been told since the day Adam's story began. However, it is not Adam's story I want to highlight in this book. It is your story that is important at this moment. It is important for you to learn the techniques of developing and sharing your story for today and into the future.

Just for the sake of having an image in our mind of what it might look like in writing our story, I want to use the analogy of using a pen and a sheet of paper. I visualize the technique in this manner: when you were born you were given a pen along with a blank sheet of paper to begin writing your journey, your life story, each step of the way. I'm not sure as you read this book when your story began, but I do know it had a beginning. My story began on February 25, 1938, and my story has been unfolding each second, minute, hour, day, week, month, year, and decade, and will continue until that day it will come to an earthly end. My reason for writing this book is to inspire you to have the same passion, curiosity, and desire I have with writing my story. This desire led me to analyzing, searching, and learning in order to help me in directing the pen that God has given me to write my story.

No matter what stage your story is in, I would like to challenge you to stop writing for a moment and learn the technique and begin the same process I did to bring me to the point I am at today. This process will carry you over the threshold of understanding and eventually bring you to the point of owning your story. Take note of the title of this book before we go any further—*Own Your Story Before Your Story Owns You.* When you cross this threshold, you will recognize how important your story is today and will be in the future. If you are not owning your story today, I hope as you read this book you will eventually arrive at that point of saying, "It is my story, and I am going to claim and own my story."

God Describes the Process of Your Life Story

Have you ever taken time to sit down with a calculator and number your days? I mean who would ever think about doing such a thing? Numbering my days had never come across my mind until one day this scripture jumped out at me and set my mind churning to learn about my story. I thought about what would be the purpose of even considering numbering my days. My question to you reading this book is, how many days have you lived? Thinking in terms of your story, just how many days have you been writing your story? It is true that we calculate our story in years. We might ask the question this way: "How old are you?" We might reply that we are seventy years old. We would never say that we are 25,550 days old. Our scripture does mention our tale or story in terms of seventy years and if by reason or strength, they are eighty years.

In Psalm 90, the Psalmist describes life in a way that we can relate to as we travel the road ahead of us. In these scriptures, he deals with the reality of life. However, it is here that causes us to slam on the brakes when it comes to owning our story. Reality defines life as it actually exists, and there are some events in our story that we would rather not own, talk about, or share. When it comes to accepting and sharing our story, we are apt to do so by painting in our minds an idealistic picture instead of a realistic picture of our story. We might highlight the good examples of our story and skip over and hide the bad and the ugly.

Let me give you a word of encouragement at this point. I realize there may be a situation that happened in your story that is more than you would want to share, so I recommend if it is too painful or if it is hurtful to others, by all means, do not share that event. Always be careful and aware of others who may be involved in an event of your story, who may need to be protected. We are inundated with reality shows on television, and we view them with a lot of excitement and anticipation, cheering on those who are excited because they are victorious and feeling a sense of reality when it comes to life. This is why it is difficult for us to own our story because it usually includes the good, bad, and the ugly.

If I would describe the reality of life God is showing us in Psalm 90, it might make each of us say, "Wow, is this all there is to my life story?" He is very pictorial in defining life for us. In paraphrasing what He is saying, I would describe life as having many good accumulating years, even though our life story is short, and we vanish away. We live our story amid God's wrath as well as His grace. There will be days and years in which you will live your idealistic story. However, there will be days in which we will be writing our story realistically while living with problems, sorrow, and pain.

It appears God is saying to us, "I know what your life is about, and I know there will be good times and bad and ugly times. Because I know the balancing act between the two idealistic and realistic poles of life and I have given you what is necessary to write your story, I will help you with the techniques of life and lead you through the processing of your life story." God is saying you probably have seventy to eighty years to write your story, and you need to count your days and use them wisely in order to experience the very best that a story can be lived in order for you to write a successful story.

God Describes How Valuable You Are to Him

> *You made all the delicate, inner parts of my body and knit me together in my mother's womb. Thank you for making me so wonderfully complex! Your workmanship is marvelous—how well I know it. You watched me as I was being formed in utter seclusion, as I was woven together in the dark of the womb. You saw me before I was born. Every day of my life was recorded in your book. Every moment was laid out before a single day had passed. How precious are your thoughts about me, O God. They cannot be numbered!*
> (Ps. 139:13–17 NLT)

It is easy to devalue your worth and the worth of your story if you do not see yourself as God sees you from the very conception of your life story. This is even before you have been given a pen and a sheet of paper to write your story on. There are many reasons why we do not see our value as described in Psalm 139:13–17. I personally believe what has created such a negative outlook concerning the value of life in our culture is the teaching of the theory of evolution in our schools and universities. I believe the theory of evolution has dumbed down the value of life in a general sense and can be seen on many levels in our current culture throughout the world. You can see it through the eyes of a horrendous act of murder by one human being upon another, committed with a seared conscience without any feeling whatsoever. You hear of killings happening upon the streets of our cities, where there are daily reports in the news of murders and violent abuse against women and children in our homes.

I believe we would see fewer abortions in our abortion clinics if people in our society would read this verse and see the minute description of what God sees in every woman's womb. Often our society is blind to the scriptural value God places upon every conception and fetus. To understand the value God has placed upon human life, one must believe man came into existence due to an intelligent cause and an intelligent design by God, the Creator of the universe. The evolutionist will disagree with this explanation and would declare that man came into existence through an undirected process of natural selection. However, it is the evolution theory that devalues the worth of a human being.

God Has Given You a Story

Now that we have focused upon the first story ever told in Adam and God's description of the process and value He has placed upon your story, it is time to begin the journey. We will break down the process of writing your story for you to claim your story, own your story, and share your story with others. Enjoy the journey set before you. God bless you as you travel.

PART 1

The Pain of Brokenness

Brokenness is a word that has been used in describing the pain and agony we experience when going through a devastating situation in our lives. My journey with brokenness opened my eyes of understanding to the special attention God gives to us in our journey of life. He is involved in every aspect of our story. Often we are afraid of the word *brokenness*, especially when referring to it in connection with a painful circumstance we are experiencing in our story. No doubt the reason is because we think of broken things being thrown away, discarded, or placed in the trash because we see no future value for anything broken. Think of a time when you dropped an expensive piece of China. Can you hear the sigh you made when you had broken a valuable article that you owned? Later you ended up throwing it away and going down to the store to buy a new one.

You see, in modern-day society, instead of fixing broken things, we throw them away. This principle is not true with God. He uses broken people to shape them into the story He wants them to become, a story that will bring glory to Him. When I was a child and started my first day of school, each year my parents bought me

1

a brand-new box of crayons as part of my school supplies. By the end of the year, most of them were broken because I would push too hard on the crayon while coloring my pictures. One thing I learned through that experience is that broken crayons still color. With that in mind, I want to share the fact that broken people can still be used by God. In this section, "The Pain of Brokenness," we will be sharing about who is in control of our story. Your story will change directions as you transfer control of your life out of your hands and into the hands of God. Let's see how this principle works in your story.

CHAPTER 1

I'm in Control

Whereas you do not know what will happen tomorrow. For what is your life? It is even a vapor that appears for a little time and then vanishes away. Instead, you ought to say, "If the Lord wills, we shall live and do this or that.
—James 4:14–15

There are many plans in a man's heart,
Nevertheless the Lord's counsel—that will stand.
—Proverbs 19:21

There is a way that seems right to a man,
but its end is the way of death.
—Proverbs 14:12

"Being in total control of our story can lead to our story being totally out of control"
—Albert Schuessler

The Early Guidance of a Parent

Being in control is a part of our human nature. The desire to be in control begins the day your story was born. Think about this very simple fact. You did not realize you wanted control or even had control when you were a baby. However, the control factor began very early in your story. Now, of course, your parents were pretty much in charge of your story at that point, but you were, in your own way, letting them know you were really in charge. After all, you were the one who determined when they got up in the middle of the night, due to your crying at the top of your lungs because you were hungry or needed to be changed.

As a baby you got familiar with a pacifier very early in your story. When you started crying for your pacifier, you sent your parents scampering for one as fast as they could to keep you quiet. You talk about control. You have seen this picture many times. Think about the time your parents were trying to shove baby food carrots into your mouth, and you took control of the situation and spit them out like a volcano. At that age, you began to learn that a temper tantrum would grab everyone's attention for you to have all of the attention. You see, control starts very early in the life of your story.

Parents play a big role in the early development of a child's story. A parent has that role, responsibility, and mandate given to them by the Word of God. I think every parent should take this mandate very seriously. God lays out the instructions in His Word exactly how to carry out His mandate. It's important as a parent to know your child and understand their temperament, talent, giftedness, and personality in order to raise them in the way they should go in developing their future story. This is to be done despite the aggravation you face in trying to control their bent to be in control. Each child, as an individual, will have different directions they will go in writing their story, according to how their inner person is made up. Parents should know each child, train them, and discipline them in the way they should go in accordance with the following scripture. *"Train up a child in the way he should go, and when he is old he will not depart from it"* (Prov. 22:6). According to the following scriptures parents are to instruct their children and teach them how to be obedient to parental authority:

> *My son, hear the instruction of your father, and do not forsake the law of your mother; For they will be a graceful ornament on your head, and chains about your neck.* (Prov. 1:8–9)

> *Children, obey your parents in the Lord, for this is right. "Honor your father and mother," which is the first commandment with promise: "that it may be well with you, and you may live long on the earth." And you, fathers, do not provoke your children to wrath, but bring them up in the training and admonition of the Lord.* (Eph. 6:1–4)

Children need this early instruction, training, and guidance for them to have a good firm foundation to launch their story at a future date. It's important for parents not only to teach their children verbally but to teach them with their behavior as well. Your children should see your story being played out in front of them. It cannot be emphasized enough the influence a parent has on their children by their actions and by the way they communicate with them. Let me state this in a pictorial way. *Give them roots and give them wings.* Give them a deeply rooted foundation and strong wings to soar high into the future while writing their story.

The Drama of a Child in Control

Most of us are aware of the famous catch phrase "the terrible twos." Yes it is at this age a child has become aware that they can have their parents chasing after them wherever they want to lead them. They have now learned how to control their parents when it comes time to go to bed at night. They now know crying seems to work in getting the attention of everyone in the house. Of course, we do not want our children to cry themselves to sleep, so we lay aside whatever we are doing and go into their bedroom to comfort them. Have you ever noticed how fast a child can stop their crying? It is a con job; they just manipulated the whole drama scene.

When they start playing with siblings and friends, playing with toys, and competing in games, you will often see children in the midst of a pile of toys, fighting over one toy. Why are they fighting over one toy when they have so many to choose from? You might hear them squabbling over the rules of a game they are playing or even cheating in some way to win the game. This drama is taking place because of control. One child or both want to be in control and are not about to give up possession of a particular toy to another child.

I think you can see the behavioral picture unfolding of human nature, even in a small child. All the commotion taking place by a two-year-old is because they have learned something about themselves that they can use in the early stage of their story. What did they learn? "I'm in control!" Each child has its own temperament and will act or react according to the control factor of that temperament. Some temperaments lean more toward control than other temperaments. Parents, I encourage you to study and learn about your child! This truth will be invaluable in the development of your child's story.

The Theatrics of a Teen in Control

When we enter the teenage years, we have a drive within us to take more control of our lives. When we were children, our parents were greatly involved in writing our story. At this point in our lives, we want to take the pen in our hands and start writing on the paper of our lives. Now we want to start flapping our wings and trying to fly. We begin exploring at an early age. We love to watch a child checking out and reaching for everything on the end table, shelves, and cabinets. But it's when we become teenagers that this same exploration turns into an adventurous endeavor, checking out things we should not be checking out. We are anxious and cannot wait until the day we can take the steering wheel and take control of the car.

This is a big moment in our lives when we are gradually becoming independent from our parents. Writing our story is crucial at this juncture of our lives. These are our high school years, and we begin to experience peer pressure from our friends. We are apt to get involved in things we know we should not get involved in, but the peer pressure is too strong for us to resist. When we succumb to this peer pressure, we are handing the pen over to the ones that are pressuring us and allowing them to write our story. You never want to get in a situation where you hand your pen to someone else to write your story. Never let someone else write your story.

Never let someone else write your story

Our Story Gradually Unfolds

Looking back, during my sixth-grade year in school, I was beginning to explore what it would be like to take more control of my story. They were not serious issues but could certainly get me into a little trouble with my schoolteacher. I was being a little mischievous in the classroom with my buddies. Often I would have to stand up against the black chalkboard with my nose in a circle that my teacher had drawn on the board with chalk. Some of my friends and I found a hiding place in the basement of our three-room schoolhouse where four of us would hide from our teacher. When we were outside in the schoolyard, we would take a little magnifying glass and, by using the sun rays, try to set grass on fire in the school yard.

In the seventh and eighth grades, I was introduced to tobacco products, and the control factor kicked in as I would explore the possibilities of smoking tobacco. Lying to my parents was easier for me to do at this age. It was less painful for me to lie than to face the consequences of my control behavior, which I thought would be more painful. I can remember going into a dime store and stealing a small package of rubber bands. When I got into our car, my father asked me where I got them. This time I did not lie and told him the truth. He took me back to the store, and I had to return them to the manager and tell him I stole them. It was painful when I told my father that I had stolen them and just as painful when I told the manager what I had done. These are a few things early in my story I am sharing with you in this book. I am sure I will share more with you as we get deeper into this book. In sharing a little of my story at this point, I am giving you a little example of what "owning your story before your story owns you" is about.

Remembering back to my teen years, while entering high school, I experienced peer pressure that I had never felt before. My parents had pretty much directed my story up to this point. They had taken me to church where I learned about sin and the consequences of sin. The Bible was taught, and I was learning about things I should and should not do according to the Word of God. My parents were reinforcing these principles into my life story as they were raising me. My mom and dad were laying the foundation of my story upon biblically moral principles and values. I realize not every child is raised upon biblical principles from a religious point of view, but I believe most parents raise their children with a desire to establish moral principles within their children's life story, based upon the consensus of a generally good and moral society

On the other side of the coin, there were many decisions I made during those same years that were good choices and actually enhanced my story. Today I can look back to my elementary and high school years and say to myself, "I'm glad I made a particular decision that was positive in my life." I can remember when I was making a bad decision that would affect my story in a negative way. In my mind, I knew it was wrong based upon what my parents had taught me. Even though I knew the decision was wrong, in the face of what my parents had taught me, I made the bad decision anyway. Why? Because at that moment I was in control and not my parents. When thinking about my story I like to call it the good, bad and the ugly. We are more than eager to share the good points about our story and tend to hide or sweep under the carpet the bad and ugly points. I decided I would cherish the good points of my story and claim the bad points and ultimately own my story.

Molded Early in Life

It is ironic that much of our story is written and molded early in life when we have never heard of or learned anything about being in control. It does not seem fair that we must go through circumstances and issues early in life that will affect us for the rest of our lives simply because we do not understand the control factor of our story. That is, however, the way stories are written. Some may have greater advantage early in life in writing their story. There are so many factors that go into story building. Factors that affect our early life, such as economics, education, location, role models, choosing friends, discipline, parenting styles, parental directions, temperament, personality, addictions, and many more factors are thrown into the pressure cooker of life to create our story. The molding of our story during the early years obviously gives us the ability to carry the control factor into our early adult life while we are choosing our higher education, profession, job selection, marriage, and having and raising children.

There are certain areas of my story, stemming from my high school years, that I did not want to own for many years—issues I carried into my early adult life from my teenage years that created some ugliness in my relationship with my wife. My reluctance to settle down in our marriage certainly caused conflict in the early stages of our relationship. This is an area in my story I had to come to grips with, claim, and own. Spending time at the bars, consuming alcohol, is a habit I brought into the marriage from my high school years that had a negative effect on our marriage, my wife, as well as our children. These areas, because of my control, very well could have had lasting damage to me, my marriage, wife, and children.

Am I pleased with my action? Absolutely not! These actions mentioned are the ugly part of my story. These are the areas that I would like to sweep under the carpet and hide. As much as I am ashamed of the lifestyle mentioned, nevertheless, they are a part of my ongoing story. Again, it was all about controlling my life and my future, not thinking about my wife or our children and their future. Gradually my life story began to turn around at the age of twenty-eight, though I was still in charge of my story.

I do not want to leave you with the impression that parenting is always the reason why many of us have some ugly scars etched into our story. The areas I shared with you that I see in my story in which I am truly ashamed of were not caused by the parenting I received from my parents. They were caused by my being in control of my life story. The things I mentioned are what I chose to do. I'm sure there are cases where parenting did play a big role in the ugly outcome of a child's story. There are so many variables in the development of our stories that at times, it may be hard to pinpoint why we did what we did. The issue is not to point fingers at anyone or anything that brought blemishes upon our story, but to claim and own what did happen in our stories.

God Gave You the Control Button

I believe one of the most remarkable aspects of God's creation of the human being is that God created man with the ability to choose. You possess the control button to write your story. He did not create us as mere puppets or marionettes with strings attached for Him to pull and yank in order for Him to make every decision for us. He did not create us as robo-humans to just look like humans but to be controlled by someone else. He could have created us in such a manner, but He chose to create us with a free will. That means we have the ability to make a choice or a decision on our own. For the sake of not getting bogged down in theology, I want to stay focused on the responsibility of people making choices. I realize there is much debate when it comes to the study of man's responsibility and God's sovereignty and how the two can work together in writing your story. I leave that debate for others to think and write about.

When Joshua was writing his story, he gave us an example of man's free will by challenging the Israelites to choose who they were going to serve. *"And if it seems evil to you to serve the Lord, choose for yourselves this day whom you will serve, whether the gods which your fathers served that were on the other side of the river, or the gods of the Amorites, in whose land you dwell. But as for me and my house, we will serve the Lord"* (Josh. 24:15). He is basically saying to them, "It is your story and the choices you make will determine how your story is going to be written. The choice you make now will also determine how future generations are going to read, write about and measure your story in the future." Joshua continues in the same scripture, telling us what his choice is going to be. "But for me and my house, we will serve the Lord." God is allowing his servant to challenge His people to be in control and to write their story accordingly. At the same time God is allowing Joshua to control the script he is writing for his story, as well. Is it your script or God's script?

Is it your script or God's script?

In the account of Adam and Eve we can see God's *will* is apparent in their story. As Satan enters the picture by joining them in writing their story, we see his influence is also apparent in their story. You might ask in what way is Satan influential? We see Adam and Eve exerting their *will* in challenging God's *will*.

> *Now the serpent was more cunning than any beast of the field which the Lord God had made. And he said to the woman, "Has God indeed said, 'You shall not eat of every tree of the garden'?" And the woman said to the serpent, "We may eat the fruit of the trees of the garden; but of the fruit of the tree, which is in the midst of the garden, God has said, 'You shall not eat it, nor shall you touch it, lest you die.'" Then the serpent said to the woman, "You will not surely die. For God knows that in the day you eat of it your eyes will be opened, and you will be like God, knowing*

good and evil." So, when the woman saw that the tree was good for food, that it was pleasant to the eyes, and a tree desirable to make one wise, she took of its fruit and ate. She also gave to her husband with her, and he ate. Then the eyes of both of them were opened, and they knew that they were naked; and they sewed fig leaves together and made themselves coverings. And they heard the sound of the Lord God walking in the garden in the cool of the day, and Adam and his wife hid themselves from the presence of the Lord God among the trees of the garden. Then the Lord God called to Adam and said to him, "Where are you?" So, he said, "I heard Your voice in the garden, and I was afraid because I was naked; and I hid myself." And He said, "who told you that you were naked? Have you eaten from the tree of which I commanded you that you should not eat?" Then the man said, "The woman whom You gave to be with me, she gave me of the tree, and I ate." And the Lord God said to the woman, "What is this you have done?" The woman said, "The erpent deceived me, and I ate. (Gen. 3:1–13)

Three Indicators That You Are in Control

Keep in mind that God created man in the image of God. He breathed into his nostrils the breath of life and man became a living soul. God in His wisdom chose to give him a *mind* to think on his own, *emotions* to share what he feels, a *conscience* to guide him morally, and a *will* to choose for himself in order to pick up the pen of life and write his story. So, the saga of the human life story began with Adam and Eve when they became the first human beings to write a life story. A portion of their story is found in the scripture before us. The story continues up to today as you write your story each moment of the day. Your story is just as important as their story was in the beginning of the human race.

Since God has chosen to interact His will with man's will, there are going to be times when they will crash at the intersection of life. There are some indicators in Genesis 3 that will reveal to us whether we are in total control of our life or if we are listening to and following God and His Word. These indicators are and will always be a part of our everyday life, to some degree, as we write our daily story. How we deal with these indicators will ultimately determine who is in control of our lives and what the end of our story will look like. Here are three principles our story writing will hinge on to determine life direction. You are encouraged to learn what they are and how God has a plan to counteract them in providing help for you in writing your story. See how Eve is going to take control of her life and ultimately Adam's life in this account.

1. *The lust of the flesh. In verse 6 she saw that the fruit was good for food.*

The *first* indicator is the lust of the flesh. It is the desire to feel physical satisfaction from activity contrary to the Word of God. The lust of the flesh draws us into sinful activity that the body craves, such as out-of-marriage activity, substance abuse, drunkenness, gossip, anger, impurity, selfish ambitions, and idolatry. Eve saw that it was good for food and would bring pleasure to the physical part of her life. The problem is that God said she was not to have the fruit of the tree. The word *flesh* in the bible is often speaking of man or animals' literal skin or flesh. The word is also used in describing our human nature or our sinful nature. Our natural state before we become believers is sometimes called the carnal part of man. In this case, the word is not speaking of something external but something internal, something within us. It's called the sin nature of man and therefore has a desire to draw us into sinful activity. If you find yourself being drawn into activities, such as mentioned above, and they are bringing pleasure to your flesh, then it might be an indicator you are in control of your life.

2. *The lust of the eye. In verse 6 she saw it was pleasant to the eye.*

The *second* indicator is the lust of the eye. It is seeing things in a way in which we covet something we should not have and is not ours. An example is seeing another person's spouse to covet them with a desire for them to be yours. Addiction to gambling could have taken place in a person's life because they coveted money and material things. In other words, the lust of the eye is the desire to have something that rightfully belongs to someone else. Eve was looking at the fruit and said, "It is pleasant to the eye." If you covet your neighbor's house, car, boat, and riches and are not satisfied with what you have, then this is an excellent indicator you are in control of your story. You are eying and coveting what someone else has accumulated.

3. *The pride of life. In verse 6 she saw that she could become wise.*

The *third* indicator is the pride of life. It is, no doubt, one of the best indicators that we are in control of our lives. Eve saw that the fruit was desirable to make one wise. Importance, prestige, power, arrogance, famous, ego, and false value are signs of pride in our story. These are all indicators you may be in control of your life.

Satan will use these three indicators to entice you to always be in total control of your life. They are indicators that are driven by the desire of our natural, carnal man. Your story has been and is being written and driven by these three factors at the forefront of your story. Some of these indicators will always be active in your natural life as you are writing your story. Keep in mind that God created you; He gave you the controls; and He gave you, in the natural state, your will to make decisions according to the flesh if you choose.

Back to our chapter title, "I'm in control," we see that control comes from various influences in our lives. God, parents, peers, authorities, inner influences, mind, emotions, will, and most of all by your own temperament, personality, and being. All these influences you have in your life will be totally different than what I have in my life and what anyone else will have in their lives. Keep in mind your story is unique.

Keep in mind your story is unique

As I conclude this chapter titled "I'm in control," you will see that in your story, there will be the good, the bad, and the ugly. This chapter is the beginning of owning your story before your story owns you. As we prepare to enter the next chapters, we will find that there will be many more aspects in the journey of writing your story. Own your story; your story is important.

Probing and Pondering, Chapter One

WRITING YOUR STORY

- Your story line in chapter 1: "I'm in control"

  *"Instead, you ought to say, "if the Lord wills,
  we shall live and do this or that"*
  —James 4:15

EXPLORE: Study the Scriptures to enhance your story line.

- *"Whereas you do not know what will happen tomorrow. For what is your life? It is even a vapor that appears for a little time and then vanishes away. Instead, you ought to say, "If the Lord wills, we shall live and do this or that."* —James 4:14–15

- *"There are many plans in a man's heart, Nevertheless the Lord's counsel—that will stand."* —Proverbs 19:21

- *"There is a way that seems right to a man, but its end is the way of death."* —Proverbs 14:12

ENGAGE: developing your story line

- *"Therefore, I say to you, do not worry about your life."* — Matthew 6:25

  1. Did your parents lay a solid foundation for your story?

  2. Were you given wings to fly, or were they clipped to keep you from flying?

3. Describe how your teenage years are now or have at some point influenced your story for good or for bad.

4. Can you think of a time when you allowed someone else to control your story?

5. Discuss a bad teenage habit you had that you carried into your adult life.

6. Where do you think your story is when it comes to the three influential indicators listed? Do you need to work on your indicators?

ENACT: applying to your story line

- *"Which of you by worrying can add one cubit to his stature?"* —Matthew 6:27

  1. What are some actions you can take to undo some of the hurt that you may have caused others?

  2. How might your parenting change in order to lay a life foundation for your child?

  3. List some ways you can overcome any of the three indicators we talked about?

EMPLOY: living out your story line

- *But by the grace of God I am what I am"* —1 Corinthians 15:10

  1. In what manner can you share your story to encourage other people?

2. What might people see in your story that you are ashamed of and need to change to share your story more effectively?

3. Owning your story will give you boldness in sharing your story in the future.

Praying for ownership: Father, I pray for understanding on how writing my story is so important. Lord, help me to realize my story is as important as anyone's story. Father, it will be difficult because of things that have happened in my past for me to own my story. God, it is my desire to begin the process of owning my story and sharing it with other people in my life as a way of encouragement to them.

CHAPTER 2

Who's in Control?

*"Where do wars and fights come from among you? Do they not come
from your desires for pleasure that war in your members?
You lust and do not have. You murder and covet and cannot obtain.
You fight and war. Yet you do not have because you do not ask."*
—James 4:1–2

*"But I see another law in my members, warring against
the law of my mind, and bringing me into captivity to the law
of sin which is in my members."*
—Romans 7:23

"When your need for control is out of control, who's in control?"
—Albert Schuessler

Recently, I was a passenger riding in a sports car, thinking it
would be a great joy ride. I thought I would be getting a sense
of what riding in a small sports car would feel like. I was excited to
get the opportunity. I had never ridden in a sports car, sitting so
low to the ground, one with a six-speed transmission and a tremendous amount of horsepower. Someone else was driving and had total
control of the car. I was a passenger with my life in the hands of the
driver. With the vehicle so low to the ground, it gave you the sense

you were going faster than you were. As we made our way into the countryside, we rounded some curves at a high rate of speed. At this point, I became a little nervous mainly because I was not in control of the sports car.

When we turned around and made our way back to the house, the driver wanted me to experience the speed of this sports car. We took off like a jet rocket, going at a high rate of speed—I mean it was fast, really fast. To be honest, I was nervous, scared, and shaking in my boots going at this speed. I experienced these feelings mainly because I was not in control of the car. It gave me the feeling which in turn triggered a question within my mind as to who's in control of this vehicle, at this speed.

The experience of the 2020 Covid 19 virus often left us feeling like we did not have control of our lives. Before the pandemic, we could pretty much go where we wanted to go and do what we wanted to do. After all, we are Americans and are free to do pretty much what we feel like doing. When the pandemic had become full scale in our country, it seemed as though we had lost control of our lives. The authorities were now saying we could not go where we wanted to go, and we could not do what we wanted to do. Restaurants, theaters, churches, schools, sports, hospitals, and other businesses were closed or locked down. Some states mandated you had to stay at home on lockdown unless you were essential to the wellbeing of people in our communities. Then there was the mandate issued by many states and counties for everyone to wear a mask while entering a place of business. Social distancing was encouraged and mandated as well. A great number of people did not like the six-foot distancing that was required while standing in line for an event. A huge segment of the population protested and defied the mask-wearing ordinances.

Not being in control of our lives as we were used to was creating various feelings and actions on our part. Some people became angry and very adamant that no one was going to tell them what to do, others became very submissive to the orders and locked themselves inside their homes for months, never to venture out into society. A number of those locked down became depressed due to their environment. The question eventually surfaced as we began to ask, "Who's in control of our lives at the present time?" Were we being controlled by our president, Congress, governors, state, county, city leader, or the CDC? Was the pandemic controlling us to the place we were paralyzed as a nation? Fear began to spread like a wildfire across our country because people were afraid of coming down with the virus and the possibility of dying from the virus. Why were we experiencing such a hopeless feeling in our nation? It is a natural feeling we have when we do not know who's in control.

Life Spinning Out of Control

You may have attended a circus or have seen a television show where someone was spinning plates. They may have ten plates spinning on different poles all at the same time. They run from one plate to another keeping the plates spinning to keep them from falling off the poles. The performer is trying to maintain control of all ten plates at the same time. During the act, it may seem like they are about to lose control of the plates and sometimes they do lose control. Suddenly one, two, or three plates quit spinning and fall to the floor. Sure enough, they lost control of the plates.

The picture of spinning plates reminds me of how our lives can begin spinning out of control. Life is meant to be lived under control. We try our best to keep up with what is going on in our lives and try to keep every aspect of our lives spinning under control,

Life is meant to be lived under control

while at the same moment, we have the feeling that our life is out of control. Life out of control is a feeling of despair. We begin to think, *no way can I keep all these plates of life spinning.* Keep in mind, control means power over, directing influence, authority to manage, ability to regulate, and capacity to hold in restraint. When life is getting out of control, we begin to lose the ability to manage our lives, we lose the influence in the direction we are moving in, we lose the ability to practice restraint, and we start doing things we know we should not be doing.

Our life spinning out of control is like a war going on inside our mind and soul. *"Where do wars and fights come from among you? Do they not come from your desires for pleasure that war in your members? You lust and do not have. You murder and covet and cannot obtain. You fight and war. Yet you do not have because you do not ask"* (James 4:1–2). James describes such an experience as a war going on inside us that has been declared by our desires for pleasure that controls all our members. Paul gives us a different picture of a life out of control. *"But I see another law in my members, warring against the law of my mind, and bringing me into captivity to the law of sin which is in my members"* (Rom. 7:23). He says a life out of control is driven by our members taking control of our minds. In other words, He is saying our minds and our souls are being taken into captivity of sin. At this point, you begin to wonder who is in control of my life.

Life out of control can happen at all stages of life. I have seen it happen in children at an early age where a devastating experience affected their lives. The death or a divorce of a parent can cause an out-of-control life experience, even for a small child. Teenagers are not exempt from undergoing painful situations that can turn their life upside down. Even at this age, a segment of their stories are being written, and they must eventually own this out-of-control period of their life. No matter what stage of life you find yourself, young adult, middle age, and the mature, you will at some time in life experience your life spinning out of control. If you have not, stick around because at some point in your story, you will be writing in detail about your out-of-control life experience. At that point, you will ask the question, who's in control?

Life: Out-of-Control Levels

In accordance with your age, you may have realized by now that life is lived at different levels. Depending on how old you are and the experiences you have had in life, you will recognize some of these levels.

Level one is when you are a child, eventually transforming into a teenager, and finally you arrive and become a young adult. These are your early ages of life when so much of your story is being written. At this age, we are experiencing the attitude of *arrogance,* and we have become egotistical, proud, self-centered, and conceited. In certain areas of this level, we are even a little *dense* in our decision-making, which means we are clueless, naive, foolish, inexperienced, and lacking in judgment. A few of the things mentioned may have been a part of your story in the past. This is the age when you are in control of your life, and no one can tell you what to do. Teen years are when life is lived at full speed.

Level two is when you are a little older and out of school and not quite as arrogant and dense in your decision-making. At this stage you are experiencing *success* and *prestige.* You have chosen a profession and are making good money as you work your way up the ladder of success. You could very well be married at this point and have bought a house with a little white picket fence neatly built around your property. You are settling in, and by now you may have a child or two. The children are active in school and love to be involved in sports, gymnastics, dance, plays, and music. On this level, you are trying to balance your time with family life, work, church, school, and running your kids to practice and eventually to the actual performance. You have become an important influence in your community, and you carry a certain amount of prestige among your peers. But wait a minute, can you feel the plates spinning and starting to get out of control? Life is moving pretty fast around the curves of life, your engine is revved up, and you are going at a high rate of speed. At this level in life, the plates are beginning to wobble, and you are getting out of breath trying to keep the plates spinning.

Level three is a stage when we sit down with ourselves and start asking some questions about our lives. This is the level of *questioning*

There is value in questioning and analyzing your life

and *analyzing.* There is value in questioning and analyzing your life. The questions are: who am I, what is my purpose in life, and what am I accomplishing with my life daily? We ask ourselves a very important question: what are my values, purpose, and direction in life? Our focus is being taken off the most important things in life, and much of what we experience at this level is trivial to our core values. At this level, we are watching the plates spin, and oftentimes they are spinning very fast and even out of control. We sit down and look at each plate and start analyzing as to why I am spinning this particular plate. We are analyzing our life because we are beginning to feel a sense of emptiness, loneliness, and helplessness. It is at this point that we begin to ask the question: who's in control?

Level four is when we realize we have lost control, and we question who's actually in control of our lives. At this level, we find ourselves experiencing *desperation* and *depression*. When we reach this point of wondering who's in control, we have come to a point of despair. I reached this point of despair in my life when I was forty-five years old when I experienced a period of depression during a painful situation. Up to this age, I was pretty much in control of my life until I found myself at the bottom of the barrel and had to ask the question, who's in control of my life. Being a stubborn and determined individual, I wanted to keep it a secret and sweep it under the carpet so no one would ever know. The depression was one of the happenings in my life that I have embraced and owned in later years. I will share the rest of my story in a later chapter in this book.

As you read this chapter, you may recognize some of the stages mentioned. I pray you will never have the experience of wondering who's in control of your life. I know our personalities, temperaments, and experiences are all different, and therefore, the degree of levels we go through will be totally different. We are not cookie-cutter human beings. Since we are not all the same, we all have different journeys of life.

Life: Out-of-Control Images

The depression I was experiencing was not clinical depression. I had never experienced depression before, nor do I today. My depression is what I call "situational depression." Two situations were taking place at the same time, causing my life to spin out of control. My perception of what was happening during this period of time was foggy. I knew my life was out of control but did not understand the technicality or mechanics of a life out of control.

I would read articles about what was happening; I would seek counsel on how to deal with and overcome the feelings of my life being out of control. I just could not see through the fog to see what was right in front of me. At this point I knew that I was not the person that I really was in life. The image I was projecting was not the true image of the person I knew that I was in life. There were times when I felt like a zombie. I was alive and moving, but I was not functioning. My countenance had fallen to the point that the real me could hardly be recognized.

I think of the story of Job in the Bible. I wonder if he ever

Why do bad things happen to good people?

thought his life was out of control. I wonder if Job ever said to himself, "Who's in control?" He was a man who loved God and had been blessed with a wonderful family and wealth, as well. As you read his story, you must ask the question: "Why do bad things happen to good people?"

> *When three of Job's friends heard of the tragedy he had suffered, they got together and traveled from their homes to comfort and console him. Their names were Eliphaz the Temanite, Bildad the Shuhite, and Zophar the Naamathite. When they saw Job from a distance, **they scarcely recognized him**. Wailing loudly, they tore their robes and threw dust into the air over their heads to show their grief. Then they sat on the ground with him for seven days and nights. No one said a word to Job, for they saw that his suffering was too great for words.* (Job 2:11–13 NLT)

How did losing his children, his wealth and his health affect this man named Job? It affected his countenance so much that his friends did not recognize him when they came to visit and give him comfort. When you read the book of Job, you are getting a glimpse of his story and one that he ultimately owns and shares. The loss of all these things happened to a man that the Bible says was a perfect and upright man, one who feared God and hated sin. Yet, look at the expression upon his face when his life is out of control. His countenance is like your countenance, or anyone would be when you have been diagnosed with cancer, served divorce papers, lost a child to death, or filed for bankruptcy. It is like all your spirit is drained out of you when you have lost control.

Job had his image exposed in the first couple verses of Job, chapter one. His image previously was one of being an upright man before God, having a great family, with a lot of money and in good health. Wow, does this sound familiar to you? Everything is going great in life; he was healthy, wealthy, and satisfied. I am in control of my story and living out my dream. My image to those around me is that I am in charge, and it just cannot get any better. Then a painful issue comes crashing down on my image, crushing it into bits and pieces, and suddenly my image changes from a happy face to a face that people

Our outward countenance can reveal our inward pain

cannot recognize. This fallen, unrecognizable countenance is a sure sign that we have lost control. Our outward countenance can reveal our inward pain.

Let's paint a picture of Job and visualize what he might have looked like before he experienced the pain of losing so much that was valuable to him. When those around Job interacted with him, I can visualize a man with a smile upon his countenance. I mean, wouldn't you have a smile upon your face if life was going quite well and you were in control of your life? When you are around your friends and neighbors, you can brag about how proud you are of your family. You would certainly have prestige in your community because of your wealth. On top of that, having a healthy body is something that will give you a pleasant countenance because you have no pain dragging you down. Even his relationship with God as described in the first few verses of the book of Job would be enough to lift one's spirit and in turn lift one's countenance. What we are seeing here is the recognizable countenance of Job before he experienced the loss of all that He owned. Then the scene changes, the expression changes, the image changes, and now Job is unrecognizable to his friends. To them, it is like *who is this man?* Well, it's the same man but an image of a man whose life is out of his control.

Sometimes we hear people say that they can do whatever they want because it does not affect anyone else but themselves. In many cases, this attitude is not so. What we do can very well affect others around us. No matter what is causing our life to spin out of control, it is in some way going to affect people that are close to us. Job's wife is a great example of what I am speaking about. I can imagine her life was moving along nicely, as well as Job's was. I'm sure there were the usual conflicts and friction in their family life from time to time. Overall, their household probably functioned in a normal way.

When bad things began happening to their family, her image changed. It was a different countenance she was now wearing on her face. *His wife said to him, "Are you still trying to maintain your integrity? Curse God and die"* (Job 2:9). Hers was not an image of depression and defeat and unrecognizable as Job's. Her response and attitude to the situation was one that triggered her emotions and set off her anger causing her to spit out bitter words such as "do you still persist in your integrity?" She continues saying to Job, "curse God and die." Can you see yourself so angry that you would advise your spouse to curse God? She got angry at God and insisted Job get angry at God as well. Can you visualize her face as you read this and focus on her countenance? Can you see the anger with the furrows in her forehead, the fire in her eyes, and the redness of her skin as her blood pressure rises to the occasion? Her countenance was very recognizable. It was a countenance of anger and rage.

Look in the Mirror at a Life Out of Control

I am sure you have looked in the mirror many times in your life, no matter how old you might be. Come on, you have looked in the mirror, and I am sure the thought came to your mind, *Hum, not bad at all*. Now that statement does not have to be driven by an ego but by the fact that I am okay with who I am. You may have stood there for quite some time, admiring the features you see in your face and in your facial expressions. While looking in the mirror, you might have tried different expressions, liking some and disliking others. The irony is that when we are in control of our lives, the facial expressions are often very pleasing to us and our friends.

When our life is spinning out of control and you look in that same mirror, you will find the countenance is not pleasing to us and unrecognizable to our friends. The question is what do you see when looking in a mirror? You probably will say, "I see myself in the mirror." That is true; you see your face and expressions, but is that really you? Looking in the mirror at yourself is not necessarily an egotistical act. Looking in the mirror can be a good and healthy way of keeping you in contact with your real self. You have heard the expression that the mirror does not lie. That is true; what you see is what you are.

I had a doctor tell me if I thought I was having a stroke to look in a mirror. He said if it was a stroke and affecting my vision, I might see one side of my face sagging, or I might see only one side of my face. He also mentioned that while I was looking directly into the mirror, by closing one eye at a time, if I were having a stroke the line across my eyes instead of being a straight line would be a zig-zagged line. Certainly, if one is thinking they are having a stroke, they need to get medical attention immediately.

Looking in a mirror can tell you many things outwardly and inwardly about your story. A mirror never lies. Being out of control, however, and not knowing who's in control is an inside depression that can show up as an outside expression. Do not overlook this aspect of your life when you feel and

A mirror never lies

have a sense you are losing control of your life. Look in the mirror at your countenance to see if it is speaking to you about the story you are writing. It is looking in the mirror that may be providing you with a defining moment in your life to accept and eventually challenge you to own your story before your story owns you. Remember Job, what was happening to him outwardly causing his life to spin out of control was affecting him inwardly and ultimately was revealed outwardly in the countenance on his face. This was his "out-of-control life" image.

Mirror, Mirror on the Wall Is God There at All?

The story of Job is a story of Satan wanting Job to deny God. It is interesting that God allowed Him to test Job in many ways, but He never allowed Satan to kill Job. Keep this in mind as you think about your life considering the message I have presented in this chapter. Though the battle between Satan and God taking place in Job's story is not your story or one you will face in a like manner, I do believe similar unseen battles do take place in our lives in the day and age in which we live. Therefore, there are times we find a battle raging in our lives, causing us to ask the question who's in control of our lives. Just as God was involved in Job's story please keep in mind that God is involved in your story, as well. You probably heard the saying, "Mirror, Mirror on the Wall Who's the Fairest of Them All?" I have found that when my life has been out of control and I am looking in the mirror and see the image of my countenance, I have asked the question: "Is God there at all?'

I encourage you to take some time with this chapter to reflect upon the title "Who's in control?" Understanding the signs of your story when out of control and the level in which you may find your life out of control is vital in owning your story before your story owns you. Reflect back to each and every level of your life and think of the signs that pointed to your life spinning out of control. When you recognize that level and at the same time you can remember the image you saw of your countenance as you looked in the mirror, you have crossed a great threshold in owning your story. As you remember that face as if it was or is a period in your life when you wondered who's in control, you can now begin to name it and claim it as your story!

Probing and Pondering, Chapter Two

WRITING YOUR STORY

- Your story line in chapter 2: "Who's in control?"

"Instead, you ought to say, "If the Lord wills,
we shall live and do this or that."
—James 4:15

EXPLORE: Study the scriptures to enhance your story line.

- *"Where do wars and fights come from among you? Do they not come from your desires for pleasure that war in your members? You lust and do not have. You murder and covet and cannot obtain. You fight and war. Yet you do not have because you do not ask"* —James 4:1–2

- *"But I see another law in my members, warring against the law of my mind, and bringing me into captivity to the law of sin which is in my members."* —Romans 7:23

ENGAGE: developing your story line

- *When your need for control is out of control, who's in control?"* —Albert Schuessler

  1. Do you have a need to be in control?

  2. How do you handle any situation where you feel you do not have control?

3. Share with others a time when you experienced your life spinning out of control.

4. With the four levels mentioned, which level is most difficult for you to go back to and own a painful experience?

5. Do you think you would react to Job's situation like Job's wife did?

6. What do you see when you look in the mirror?

ENACT: applying to your story line

- *"When your need for control is out of control, who's in control?"* —Albert Schuessler

  1. What steps can you take to begin the journey of owning your story?

  2. If you see your countenance has fallen when looking in the mirror, what might you do to fix that countenance?

  3. Make a list of ways you might take to stop your life from spinning out of control.

EMPLOY: living out your story line

- *"When your need for control is out of control, who's in control?"* —Albert Schuessler

  1. Share with others as to why your life is spinning out of control.

  2. Own your countenance and do not be ashamed of your life being out of control.

3. Encourage others when you see their countenance has fallen and they are going through a painful experience with their life spinning out of control.

Praying for ownership: Father, I ask You to help me in those times when I feel like my life is spinning out of control. I pray You will grow me spiritually as I journey through any painful experience that I might face. Lord, as I look in the mirror every day, may I not only see my face, but may I see the face of Jesus in the mirror to encourage me. Father, I ask you to challenge me in making changes in my life and to encourage me to come alongside others when their lives are out of control. Lord, empower me to overcome the desire to always be in control of my life and every situation.

CHAPTER 3

God's in Control

*"For I know the plans I have for you," says the Lord. "They are plans
for good and not for disaster, to give you a future and a hope."*
—Jeremiah 29:11 NLT

*"Trust in the Lord with all your heart and lean not on your own
understanding; In all your ways acknowledge Him,
And He shall direct your paths."*
—Proverbs 3:5–6

"God who controls the vast universe is surely
capable of controlling our fast universe"
—Albert Schuessler

If you recall, part 1 of this book is titled "The Pain of Brokenness."
Up to this point, you have been on your journey of life, writing
your story. You started the journey in a natural way—being in control of your life—especially after reaching a certain age. If your life
is like most lives, you could very well have experienced a fun and
exciting life of adventure. There may have been some rough spots,
some valleys, some sharp curves, some mountains to climb, and possibly some quicksand to escape from before you sank. Everyone is

going to face a few unpleasant obstacles. You faced them and moved on with your story into new chapters of life.

You see, it is not wise to measure your life by one or two unpleasant experiences when you have had a fulfilling life outside of those experiences. You must take time to remember and cherish those occasions where you excelled in life when you were doing a great job being in control of your life. Keep in mind that your life is important and valuable, and as our chapter verse states, God has a plan for your life. I don't know about you, but I get excited when I begin to think that there is a story already planned out for me by the God of this universe. Yes, God has a plan for you. Right now, let your mind gravitate back to those very special occasions in your story that were so exciting and fulfilling. Claim those times and own them as a part of your story to be shared with others as a way of encouragement to them.

I want the journey through this book to be a positive experience for the reader. Even the negative painful experiences we shared in chapter two, using Job as an example, are to be viewed in a positive light. When you realize God has a plan for your life and it is a plan for your good and not a disaster, one that gives you hope, you can rest assured He is involved in every aspect of your story. In order to live through a painful event and come out on the other side a better person rather than a bitter person will be dependent upon the fact that you understand God's inner workings in your life during the ordeal you are facing. I believe this is why Job did not curse God during his painful event, even though his wife insisted he do so.

Living in the Parenthesis

The chapter two experience of not knowing who is in control of our lives is what I call living in the parenthesis of life. A pair of parentheses is used to mark off an interruption of continuity in a sentence. In writing, parentheses separate one thought from another in the same sentence with brackets. In the Latin and Greek languages, the word means to "set aside" or "put aside." In a sentence, you write a thought, you then put it aside with a parenthesis with a different thought, and then you come back after the parenthesis continuing with your original thought. Applying the principle of a parenthesis to life experiences would look something as follows: you are in control of your life and things are continuing along rather smoothly; then suddenly a painful situation enters your life. It could be failing health, financial bankruptcy, or a fighting divorce, causing havoc with your life. These experiences put a halt to the continuity of your life. We are stymied with anxiety, depression, turmoil, fear, the unknown, and life comes to a halt. We are not functioning like we were before these things hit us hard. It's like your life is "set aside" for a period until you work through these matters. It's as though your life is in parentheses during this stage. This parenthetical period is when you realize you are not in control of your life. Your life will stay in this "set-aside" parenthesis stage until you work through your pain and come out on the other side to continue with your life as it was before you entered your parenthesis. Think back to a time when a part of your life was set aside by a parenthesis that was inserted in the journey of your life. I call it when life halts between the brackets.

When life halts between the brackets

Brokenness in the Parenthesis

Becoming familiar with the term *brokenness* is paramount to understanding more clearly what God is doing during those times when your life is in a parenthesis. Brokenness is defined as something that is torn, fractured, out of working order, or broken into pieces. I understand that the word can mean different things to different people for different circumstances. It could mean a broken bone, a broken crayon, a broken dish, a broken TV, a broken marriage, a broken contract, a broken trust, or a broken heart. Since we live in a throw-away society when it comes to broken things, we often just throw them away and buy a new one. If it is a broken bone, a broken marriage, a broken tooth, or a broken trust, we make an attempt to repair and mend them, so they are in working order and able to function again. You can think of a lot of ways to use the word *broken* because you have had many things that have been broken in your lifetime. The brokenness I am speaking of is more an inside job than an outside job.

Understanding Life in the Parenthesis

I want to narrow down the definition of brokenness to have a greater understanding of the true meaning of brokenness taking place in our lives. I want to present it in a way that we see and understand brokenness, not so much in the physical realm, but we see and understand it in the spiritual realm, which in turn can affect the physical. Spiritual brokenness can create physical brokenness. We must see brokenness taking place deep inside our soul and spirit. These two are the deepest and most complex parts of who we are. Our spirit is the engine that drives our spiritual life and allows us to have a relationship with God. When we become a believer in Christ, our spirit, which was dead, is now regenerated and comes alive. This is what the Bible calls being "born again."

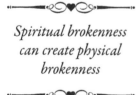

Spiritual brokenness can create physical brokenness

Our spirit is what separates us from the animal world since they are not capable of establishing a spiritual relationship with God. Likewise, our soul consists of our mind, emotions, and will and is the engine that drives our life as it relates to ourselves and to other people through our intelligence and thinking ability. You see, human intelligence is in contrast to animal instinct. As mentioned before, the brokenness I am speaking about is what I call an inside job. It is in the heart, the soul, and the spirit as defined in the Word of God. *"For You do not desire sacrifice, or else I would give it; You do not delight in burnt offering the sacrifices of God are a broken spirit, A broken and a contrite heart—These, O God, You will not despise"* (Ps. 51:16–17).

These verses speak of brokenness in our spirit and in our heart. It speaks of a contrite heart; in the original language *contrite* means to collapse or break. Therefore, these verses are talking about a broken spirit, a broken heart, or a broken person on the inside. It's important when speaking of a broken spirit that we are not thinking of it in the sense that God wants to break our spirit or our will. Spiritual brokenness is not like what we know as breaking a horse. When we think of breaking a wild horse, running the range, we are talking about breaking the spirit of that horse by putting a saddle on its back and a bit in its mouth. We then are going to mount the horse by swinging into the saddle, grabbing the reins, and having full control of the horse. The title of this chapter is "God's in Control." In using this statement of God in control, I want to leave a clear understanding that it is not the same as someone in control of a horse. The means and the purpose of a person being in control of a horse and of God being in control of a person are totally opposite.

God in the Midst of the Parenthesis

The picture of the sailors and the ships that go out into the deep waters in the following verses is a good definition and a picture of spiritual brokenness that allows God to control our lives.

> *Those who go down to the sea in ships, who do business on great waters, they see the works of the Lord, And His wonders in the deep. For He commands and raises the stormy wind, which lifts up the waves of the sea. They mount up to the heavens, they go down again to the depths, Their soul melts because of trouble. They reel to and fro, and stagger like a drunken man, and are at their wits' end. Then they cry out to the Lord in their trouble, And He brings them out of their distresses. He calms the storm, so that its waves are still. Then they are glad because they are quiet; So, He guides them to their desired haven.* (Ps. 107:23–30)

Verse 27 speaks about the sailors' dilemma in deep waters and says, "and are at their wits' end." This seems to be the point of brokenness in their lives when God steps in to take control and helps them through the deep waters. There are so many points of reference concerning brokenness in these verses that tell a story within themselves. I can imagine that you, the reader, at some point in your life, when a painful situation caused you to feel like you were in deep waters and treading water for your life, you may have said under your breath, "I am at wit's end." Let's bring the definition of brokenness into focus through this biblical picture of wit's end. When we are at wit's end, we are saying "I am puzzled, I am perplexed and baffled, and I do not know what to do next with the situation I am facing."

It's being in a state of distress, wondering if you have enough mental stamina to continue in this parenthesis moment.

The word *wit* in the original language means wisdom, skillful, or wise. When we are broken and at wit's end means we don't have the wisdom or the skill to function normally, and therefore we need God's control in helping us through our parenthesis journey. It's important that we are willing to own our *wit's end* since it's an important part of our story. In many cases, it's the most influential part of our life story. Do not neglect your wit's end or sweep it under the carpet, but rather, claim it even though it may have been the most painful segment of your journey to date.

I am intrigued with the story found in Psalm 107:23–30 that reminds me of Christians who are willing to journey out into the deep sea with God and do business with Him. It makes it clear that it is not putting your feet in the shallow waters where you will see the wonders of God, but rather casting yourself into the deep water. However, keep in mind, it is stormy in the deep waters where the waves thrust high into the air, and then they fall deep into the waters and create trouble for the sailors. As a matter of fact, they experience so much turmoil in the deep sea that they know not what to do and eventually come to wit's end. This is a pivotal point in their story and will be a pivotal point in your story as well. They find themselves in a parenthesis, they are being broken, they have lost control, they are scared, they do not know what to do other than to cry out to God for help. I imagine some of you may have rocked in the boat with these sailors at some point in your life.

I've come to the conclusion that, in many cases, it's a good place to be, though very painful, because we are transitioning from controlling our lives to allowing God to be at the helm of our story. The parenthesis that we've been talking about and many of you, if not all, have or are experiencing defining moments in your lives. Defining moments are those moments in our lives when something major took place and our lives were changed. However, we tend to hide and not claim those defining moments as a part of our life story. Then, later in life, they become a hindrance in our relationships. They haunt us and often create a low self-esteem feeling about who we are. Why? Because we were not willing to own them. Thus, we must own our story before our story owns us.

To continue our story, we see in verses 28–30 that God brings them out of their distress, He calms the storm, the waves become still, they are glad, and they are quiet. Now because God is in control, He guides them to their destination and out of their parenthesis. Drama disappears when God appears. Our chapter verse says

Drama disappears when God appears

God has a plan for us for good and not for disaster and a plan to give us a future and a hope. The amazing thing about your parenthesis moment is when you begin to realize God is working out His plan in the midst of your life's brokenness. It is at this point that you begin to sense that God is in control in your darkest hour at a time when you wondered who was in control. As far as you were concerned, your life was out of total control. Knowing that God is in control of your life at a point when it seems it is out of control is an important factor that will help you own your story. If we don't know and accept this factor, we will never own our story; on the contrary, our story will own us.

A Man Paralyzed by His Parenthesis

Elijah's story is a great illustration of how God works amid our brokenness. The following scriptures give in detail the life story of a man named Elijah who found himself in a parenthesis of life that literally paralyzed him from functioning in a normal way. When your life comes to a halt. Take time to read his story and see the struggle he had in accepting and owning his story to the extent that he came to his wit's end. Here is this great prophet of God sitting under a broom tree, depressed and ready to die. Elijah was a man that the Bible says was taken up into heaven by a chariot of fire. He wanted to give up on life early, however. I see Elijah who had pretty much been in control of his life up to this point now sitting under this broom tree, wondering who was in control. In his eyes and in his mind, he obviously thought Jezebel was in control. She was, however, not in control as we will see when dissecting this portion of scripture in its context. What we get is a glimpse of God, in the midst of Elijah's parenthesis, taking control of his life. I want the reader to see how God does this and to realize as you go through your parenthesis valley, God will be working in your life as well. His work in your case will be much like it was in Elijah's life to bring Elijah out of his parentheses in order for Elijah to move on with his life story into the future.

> *And Ahab told Jezebel all that Elijah had done, also how he had executed all the prophets with the sword. Then Jezebel sent a messenger to Elijah, saying, "So let the gods do to me, and more also, if I do not make your life as the life of one of them by tomorrow about this time." And when he saw that, he arose and ran for his life, and went to Beersheba, which belongs to Judah, and left his servant there. But he himself went a day's journey into the wilderness and came and sat down under a broom tree. And he prayed that he might die, and said, "It is enough! Now, Lord, take my life, for I am no better than my fathers!" Then as he lay and*

slept under a broom tree, suddenly an angel touched him, and said to him, "Arise and eat." Then he looked, and there by his head was a cake baked on coals, and a jar of water. So, he ate and drank, and lay down again. And the angel of the Lord came back the second time, and touched him, and said, "Arise and eat, because the journey is too great for you." So, he arose, and ate and drank; and he went in the strength of that food forty days and forty nights as far as Horeb, the mountain of God. And there he went into a cave, and spent the night in that place; and behold, the word of the Lord came to him, and He said to him, "What are you doing here, Elijah?" So he said, "I have been very zealous for the Lord God of hosts; for the children of Israel have forsaken Your covenant, torn down Your altars, and killed Your prophets with the sword. I alone am left; and they seek to take my life." Then He said, "Go out, and stand on the mountain before the Lord." And behold, the Lord passed by, and a great and strong wind tore into the mountains and broke the rocks in pieces before the Lord, but the Lord was not in the wind; and after the wind an earthquake, but the Lord was not in the earthquake; and after the earthquake a fire, but the Lord was not in the fire; and after the fire a still small voice. (1 Kgs 19:1–12)

God Controlling the Parenthesis

Handing over the control of our lives is a fearful proposition. However, keep in mind the old saying "We have nothing to fear but fear itself." No doubt Elijah was filled with fear and was afraid

Jezebel was going to take his life. Let me suggest why we need not fear when God is in control of our lives. The brokenness that takes place in our parenthesis brings us to the point of wit's end. Notice in 1 Kings 19:4, Elijah said, "It is enough," which describes coming to wit's end. At this point we must not see God taking over the control of our lives like a horseman taking control of a horse. We do not see God taking over the control of the sailors in such a manner in our scripture. We know what it is like when we are in control of our lives. We certainly know what it's like when our lives are out of control.

Now let's see what it's like when God is in control of our lives. It means we yield to His guidance in giving us direction through our parenthesis in life. We rely upon His wisdom in all the decisions we make. We draw from His power in order to accomplish life itself. We lean upon His love to provide comfort for our aching hearts. We trust in His grace to quiet our minds by eliminating the obsessive thoughts which are driving us to wit's end. We surrender to His omniscience, omnipotence, and omnipresence for the victory in living His planned destination for us. This my friend is what is meant by God is in control.

You can see a transition of control taking place while Elijah is sitting under the broom tree. God is going to minister to Elijah during his time of depression and brokenness. I want to point out that no matter who you are, what you are going through or how much pain you are experiencing right now, God is ministering to you as well. You may not realize He is in the midst and controlling your story during your darkest hour. I know you may be thinking, where in the world is God when I am going through my valley of brokenness and need Him the most.

Not only were these my thoughts, where is God, but these thoughts stimulated anger in me toward God during this most painful time in my story. I want you to know as a part of owning my story was to admit that I was wrong, I should have known better. I have asked God to forgive me for that anger. I learned the lesson well, God was in the midst of my story and humbling me to the point of relinquishing my control to Him. What is so amazing about God is even though He is in control He gives me the privilege of still being myself and utilizing my personality, my temperament, my talents, and my gifts to continue writing my story. He is not riding me like a person rides a horse to take full control of the animal. On the contrary, He is in the midst of my life providing direction, wisdom, love, grace, and strength for the journey to fulfill His plan.

Notice how God ministered to Elijah. When you are at wit's end you will be extremely tired most of the time similar to Elijah. God sent an angel to care for him. The angel touched him and said arise and eat. You see, it may be your guardian angel, your special angel that will be ministering to you during your difficult time. I cannot think of a force that is going to lift you up and carry you through your dark hour that could be greater than the touch of God upon your life.

No doubt this is God's way of saying to Elijah, "Everything is okay. You are not in control of your situation right now, but I am in control." The angel had set a cake baked on coals and a jar of water next to him. The angel came the second time with the message saying, "Your story is not yet complete. Your journey is too great for you to be in control." So, Elijah rose and ate the food. God provided enough food and drink to give Elijah the strength to make the journey of forty days and forty nights. The message of Elijah's story is that you are not going through your valley alone. God is in the midst and in control of your situation. Rise up from your brokenness because your journey is too great for you to make the journey by yourself. Allow God to be in control in writing the rest of your story. God has something great for you to accomplish in the future.

Eliminating the Parenthesis

With God in control, the parentheses come to an end, and now you can get back to living life and writing your story as God intended. The only difference with your story now being written is the one directing the pen while writing your story. It is not you in control, but now God has control of the pen. God's hand is steady and doesn't shake. When you get past the parenthesis, it is still your story being written with your personality, your temperament, your talents, your gifts, your abilities, your intellect, and your total being. He did not take that away from you as mentioned before to be in control of your life. Even though the parenthesis is over, the pain of your situation is now going to be in the past, you must remember when the special time comes, you will need to deal with and own this parenthesis of your story. By doing so you will draw attention to God's deliverance and give Him the glory for what He has done in your life. You will own your story instead of your story owning you. This is a great threshold to pass over in finding victory in your life. I hope and pray Part 1, "The Pain of Brokenness," has been a blessing to you in facing your parenthesis.

God's hand is steady and doesn't shake

Probing and Pondering, Chapter Three

WRITING YOUR STORY

- Your story line in Chapter 3: "God's in Control"

"Instead, you ought to say,
"If the Lord wills, we shall live and do this or that."
—James 4:15

EXPLORE: Study the scriptures to enhance your story line.

- *"For I know the plans I have for you," says the Lord. "They are plans for good and not for disaster, to give you a future and a hope."* —Jeremiah 29:11 NLT

- *"Trust in the Lord with all your heart And lean not on your own understanding; In all your ways acknowledge Him, And He shall direct your paths."* —Proverbs 3:5–6

ENGAGE: developing your story line

- *"God who controls the vast universe is surely capable of controlling our fast universe."* —Albert Schuessler

  1. Discuss a time in your life when you felt like you were at wit's end.

  2. Share with your group a parenthesis moment in your life?

  3. Discuss your understanding of brokenness being an inside job.

4. Write down any thoughts you might have about God being in control.

5. Share the picture you have in your mind of God being in control of your life that may be a different picture than what I shared in this chapter.

6. Can you relate to Elijah sitting under the broom tree? Discuss with others.

ENACT: applying to your story line

- *"God controls the universe; will he keep your boat afloat in the stormy sea?"*

  1. What steps can you take to turn over the steering wheel of your life to Him?

  2. Does knowing how God ministered to Elijah help you in trusting God with your parentheses?

  3. Would you be more apt to step out into the deep waters of life at the present, knowing God will quiet the storm as he did in the case of the sailors?.

  4. Is accepting the fact God is in control help you to own your story today?

EMPLOY: living out your story line

- *"When people see you, who would they think was in control of your story?"*

  1. Share with others that part of your story that was set aside by a parenthesis.

2. Can you be like the sailors and Elijah giving God the glory for your brokenness?

3. Encourage others by overcoming your fear of brokenness and share with them how you overcame that fear.

4. Share with others your desire to have God in control of your journey.

Praying for ownership: Father, I ask You to help me in the times when I fear the painful situations in my life. I need You to minister to me when I find myself at wit's end. I pray You will grow me spiritually as I journey through any painful experience that I might face in the future. Lord, my desire is to see more clearly God's working within my life. I pray I will be able to turn over the control of my life for God to fulfill His plan for my life. Inspire me to share my "that is enough" moment with others as a means of encouragement to others. God, I trust You when it comes to the "inside job" of brokenness in my life.

PART 2

The Beauty of Transformation

I n Part Two of this book, we are going to be sharing with you about what is taking place in the brokenness stage of your life. What is materializing in this set-aside parenthesis you are experiencing? What is the result of brokenness in your life, what does it produce, and what is the final outcome of brokenness? Is the after effect of brokenness worth going through your painful ordeal? Is it going to make any difference in your life? Will you be a better person after you have made the journey and come out on the other side of the parenthesis? What will you look like? Will there be significant changes made in your inner person, in your soul and spirit, that will be noticeable in your outer appearance?

We are going to look to nature to find the answer to these questions. In this case we are going to be looking at the insect world. God oftentimes refers to nature to paint a picture to help us in understanding spiritual principles and applications. He directs our attention to several insects, such as flies, ants, gnats, locusts, grasshoppers, and bees to name a few. We are going to picture the transformation of a caterpillar into a butterfly to assist you in understanding the process of spiritual brokenness that is happening in your story. The butterfly has gone through a process of transformation that involves a parenthesis of darkness, pain, and loneliness that ultimately produces light, healing, and beauty. I want to help you unfold your understanding so you can clearly see the process of natural and spiritual transformation. In this part, we answer the question of what you will look like after your brokenness. Will others see the beauty of your brokenness? Will others see the change God has made in your life through His transforming power? I believe they will.

CHAPTER 4

The Caterpillar

"But we all, with unveiled face, beholding as in a mirror the glory of the Lord, are being transformed into the same image from glory to glory, just as by the Spirit of the Lord."
—2 Corinthians 3:18

"Among whom also we all once conducted ourselves in the lusts of our flesh, fulfilling the desires of the flesh and of the mind, and were by nature children of wrath, just as the others. But God, who is rich in mercy, because of His great love with which He loved us, even when we were dead in trespasses, made us alive together with Christ (by grace you have been saved."
—Ephesians 2:3–5

"Brokenness is the pain; transformation is the gain."
—Albert Schuessler

"Transformation is a change in our lives produced by an exchange with Christ's life."
—Albert Schuessler

In the last few chapters, I have been sharing my thoughts about brokenness. We have learned that brokenness is a very real experience in our stories. Not only is it real, but it is very difficult to wrap our minds around in understanding. Brokenness is one of those experiences that, at the end of the day, we scratch our heads and say, "What just happened to me?" In the next few chapters, we are going to discuss the principles of transformation. Transformation is much like brokenness when it comes to wrapping our minds around their definition and principles. When you experience these two principles at work in your life you are in for a great challenge

Brokenness is the pain, while transformation is the gain

and a change in the direction of your life story. Brokenness is the engine that drives the train of transformation down the tracks of life in your story. It appears the two like hanging out together in our lives. When you see one you usually see the other one. Brokenness is the pain, while transformation is the gain.

Transformation regains the light that brokenness has stolen from our story. The two vary in distance from each other. For some, it may take many months or years for transformation to appear out of our brokenness. For others, it may be only a matter of days for the transformation to be experienced in our lives. Brokenness gives God the control of our lives, and He is the one that directs our lives toward and through transformation. But what exactly is spiritual transformation, and how can it occur in our lives? To help us understand, let us look at a common real-world, physical transformation: the journey a caterpillar takes to become a butterfly.

Transformation Defined

Most dictionaries define transformation as a "thorough, complete, and dramatic change in a person or in an object's appearance or form." In other words, transformation is a process of change. When it comes to our personal lives, sometimes that change can be dramatic. When the change comes through the hand of God, it will be a thorough and complete change. Let's consider the caterpillar; it changes form and appearance into a butterfly. In other words, the process by which this change takes place is called transformation. In looking at transformation from a human aspect, we will consider how God can change a Christian's secular life that looks like the world into a Christian's spiritual life that looks like Christ. Transformation is the formation of a new life.

Transformation is the formation of a new life

God's desire is for us to appear like Christ in all that we say and do. This principle we see in our chapter verse where it says, *"But we all, with unveiled face, beholding as in a mirror the glory of the Lord, are being transformed into the same image from glory to glory, just as by the Spirit of the Lord."* As brokenness unfolds in our lives and we reach a point where we succumb to its influence, we then come to the point of yielding our lives to God. It is at this juncture that God is able to use our experience by drawing us closer to Him in person and appearance. He has predestined us to be conformed to the image of His son.

The apostle Paul points out this principle in Romans 8:28–29 where he says, *"And we know that all things work together for good to those who love God, to those who are called according to His purpose. For whom He foreknew, He also predestined to be conformed to the image of His Son, that He might be the firstborn among many brethren."* Paul is encouraging us in our brokenness and parenthesis by stating that whatever we are facing in our life journey, God can leverage that moment into something good and use it to fashion our lives into the image of Christ.

Transformation Pictured

Do you believe people can change? Do you believe that you can change? Don't answer this question right now; wait until you get to the end of the book to answer the question. The reason I asked the question here is for you to think about transformation taking place in your life and for you to consider the possibility of it being a part of your story. However, it is important for us to have a picture in our mind as to what transformation is and what the process of this change taking place is. Knowing the definition and process might be helpful in how you answer the question. Metamorphosis is the Greek word that paints a beautiful picture for us of what transformation looks like. It is a process in the insect world that pictures an insect changing from an immature form to an adult form in stages.

The apostle Paul used this picture in Romans 12:2, *"And do not be conformed to this world, but be transformed by the renewing of your mind, that you may prove what is that good and acceptable and perfect will of God."* Additionally, he used it in 2 Corinthians 3:18, *"But we all, with unveiled face, beholding as in a mirror the glory of the Lord, are being transformed into the same image from glory to glory, just as by the Spirit of the Lord."* By using the example of metamorphosis in describing transformation, Paul adds another picture for you to look at in helping you understand the changes you go through in life.

You are familiar with what an electric transformer does while sitting on an electric pole or in a box near your house. A transformer takes the electricity of a high voltage power line crisscrossing the country or those underground in the cities and changes the voltage into a lower voltage coming into your house for your appliances to operate safely. In this case, the transformation is from high voltage to a lower voltage.

My prayer is that the answer to the question will be clear as we near the end of the book. I emphasize the transformational journey of your story because it is such a beautiful picture of what God can do with our lives when we relinquish control of our lives and allow God to be in charge.

Awkward Stage of a Caterpillar

The caterpillar is the awkward stage of metamorphosis. It may not be the darkest stage nor the most beautiful stage; it is simply an awkward stage. Caterpillars do not have bones in their body, which makes them unique. I love the color that God has given to the animal and insect world. He certainly went out of His way in providing color to the many varieties of caterpillars. I am fascinated by their slinky-like movement, creeping and crawling, while watching them move from one point to another on the ground or on a plant. I love to watch little children being intrigued when they see a caterpillar. It could very well be the color, slinky movement, or the fuzzy outer portion that draws a child's attention to a caterpillar.

As you watch the locomotion of a caterpillar, you wonder how long it will take to get to its destination. There is movement, and it looks like fast movement, but the distance of that movement seems like an eternal mile. The slinky movement of a caterpillar begins with what scientists call a gut movement, the gut being near the front of the caterpillar's body. The gut lunges forward even before the middle prolegs move forward. The rear prolegs then move forward, and eventually the back half of the body would catch up and slide over the gut, moving the caterpillar forward. Certainly, the caterpillar and the way it is able to crawl is a beautiful picture of the mind and hand of God in His marvelous creative action.

The caterpillar enters this world by eating its way out of the egg that was laid by a female monarch butterfly on a leaf attached to a limb. They live their entire short life, eating and growing. They often are called an "eating machine" because they come into this world hungry, hungry, hungry, and they eat, eat, and eat. They have a strong appetite that lasts through the fulfillment of the caterpillar stage. They mostly chow down on the milkweed plant. The milkweed is poisonous because it contains several substances called cardenolides that are toxic. The monarch caterpillar not only eats from this toxic plant but stores some of the toxin in its body as a defense system against certain birds. It is an amazing fact that it can eat this poisonous milkweed and live.

Once the caterpillar has eaten its fill, it will find a branch and hang upside down from that branch and go into the next stage, which is called the cocoon. Before it goes into that stage and is still a caterpillar, it provides us with a few similarities of what the metamorphosis journey looks like in human form.

Human Survival of the Awkward Stage

As you begin life and start writing your story, it begins in the awkward stage of childhood and adolescence. We will see many similarities in comparing our early life to that of a caterpillar. The caterpillar stage is generally thought of as the immature stage of the insect order called Lepidoptera. It is an important stage, but it is not as glamorous as the latter stage called the butterfly.

Most of us can remember back to when we were kids and would often find ourselves in an awkward situation. This seemed especially true when we were interacting with adults. Adults sometimes forget we were just kids, and not knowing everything they knew, we found ourselves acting in a way in which we did not seem very intelligent.

As a child, when you were with adults and they were in conversation, it seemed very awkward listening to them for a period of time, and all you could do was sit there and pay attention. You were probably thinking it would not be so awkward if I could just go off and play a game or do something that was productive.

When you finally reached the stage of adolescence, the awkwardness seemed more profound. Here you were interacting as much with your peers as you were with your parents and other adults. You can remember how you looked and how awkward you walked in your junior high days. It seemed at times you were clumsy, tripping over your own feet. It was like you stumbled into the classroom the first day of your junior high year. You were praying no one saw you in this awkward state. Go back and look at some of the pictures in your junior high and senior high yearbooks. Look at the glasses you were wearing and your hairstyle. Look at the goofy clothes you might have picked out to wear on picture day. At this age, you were at the awkward stage of meeting the opposite sex for the first time. Up to this point, you cared little about the opposite sex, but now you have an interest and have no idea on how to approach them to strike up a conversation. When the girls would like a special boy, they would smile, look pretty, and giggle as they were walking by or approaching a boy. On the other hand, when a boy would like a girl, he would walk with a swagger like some famous cowboy in a Western movie, flexing his muscles as he approached the girl.

Keep in mind that this awkward stage was the very first part of your life story being written. This stage of your story is much like the caterpillar, slinking along slowly, fulfilling the first stage of his life story and his first glimpse of transformation. This was our start, and despite this awkward stage, it was the stage where we were fumbling our way into taking control of our lives.

Curbing the Appetite

There is one thing we have learned about the caterpillar, and that is its appetite is active the minute it eats its way out of the egg and continues until they attach themselves upside down to a limb, waiting to transform into their next stage of life. The caterpillar is noted for its humongous appetite. Eating and eating is all it thinks about in life. It grows larger and larger and larger very quickly.

In our early stages of writing our story and wanting to oversee its content, we find our lustful appetite is one component that drives our story at this point. *"For all that is in the world—the lust of the flesh, the lust of the eyes, and the pride of life—is not of the Father but is of the world."* (1 John 2:16)

Lust is an inherent part of our lives from birth until we die. It is a part of the sin nature we inherited at birth due to the fall of mankind as recorded in Genesis chapter three. The Bible speaks of lust many, many times throughout its pages. It is the sinful power or influence within that part of us the Bible calls the flesh. In the previous verse, it is called the "lust of the flesh" and the "lust of the eye" and defined as the reason pride will go to seed in our lives. A simplified definition of lust could be stated as a longing for what is forbidden. More familiar words that could describe lust would be craving, desires, passion, and appetite. A craving would be like longing for a piece of chocolate. Desire is a feeling one would have for something that gives us joy or satisfaction. Passion is a strong and almost uncontrollable emotion, such as strong sexual desires driven by lust. Appetite is a strong desire and longing of satisfaction for such things as hunger, thirst, and sexuality. *"and those who are in the flesh, living a life that caters to sinful appetites and impulses, cannot please God"* (Rom. 8:8, AMP).

Catering to the lust, passion, and appetites is certainly not pleasing to God. What is so interesting is that most of us in the early awkward stage of our stories do not realize that the appetite we are feeding is not pleasing to God. We get caught up in peer pressure, and we do sinful things ignorantly at times. Lust is when all of these are combined into one and lures us into sinful activity. Thinking back to our preteen, teen, and early adult life, I am sure many of us can relate to these words when it comes to writing our stories. The influence of this appetite to affect our minds with sinful thoughts may have been very real during this time of our lives. As we grew out of the awkward stage, often that influence would entice us to act in ways that we knew were wrong and sinful. As we grew older and reached an age where we stopped the merry-go-round of life for a few minutes and took inventory of our lives, we realized that much of our heartache, hurt, pain, and disappointment happened during this period of writing our stories. There are many things written on the pages of our lives that were created by these appetites, and they are things we must own. If we do not own them, they will come back and haunt us some day, and at that time, our story will then own us.

In a great number of cases, as we were living life like the caterpillar with our humongous appetite to live a sinful life, we finally matured. Many of you were able to curb your sinful appetite as you became wiser. Somewhere along the journey, you realized your story needed to change or there was a painful circumstance happening within your story that was instrumental in your life's story change of directions. To curb your appetite is to halt the power of sin.

To curb your appetite is to halt the power of sin

In my own case, I had brought many of my teenage appetites into my early adulthood and into my marriage. The story I had written up to that period of time was filled with the consequences of my fleshly appetite. Yes, there is page after page in my life story that I had to eventually own. I really did not mature until my mid-twenties, and at that time, I began to curb some of these appetites. It was not until my mid-forties that my life story did a complete turnaround and headed in a new and fresh direction due to the transformation God brought about in my life.

I have often wondered in my own mind as to why at the earlier and awkward stages of our life story that our appetites have such a strong and powerful drive within us to the extent that so much damage to our story is done during this period. You may be reading this book and may be saying to me, under your breath, "Not me. I never gave into the appetites, passion, cravings, or desires you have described." If that is you, I would simply say to you be very thankful and thank God that the sinful acts driven by lust cannot be found upon the pages of your life story. Having said that, because of the experience of pastoring people for over fifty years, I would have to say I know very few people who have not experienced the hurts and pain of youthful appetites.

Coming back to the phrase, "eating machine," I call the caterpillar; it can never curb its appetite. Its appetite is its life and for all its life. All it knows at this stage of its life is to eat. The caterpillar can try to fly, but not yet, for its appetite is holding it back. You see, the caterpillar cannot fly until it is transformed. We, like the caterpillar, cannot become what God would have us to become until we curb the appetite and turn loose of the control of our lives. Much like the caterpillar, when we mature into various stages of life, that's when change can take place. The problem we have is in our early lives when we are much like the caterpillar, we are being driven and controlled by our appetites. Therefore, it is important to learn early in life, and if we have children to teach them and help them to learn how to curb appetites. If we do so, it will protect us from a lot of the hurt and pain that we find in so many early chapters of so many people.

Losing Control of Control

The secret to curbing the fleshly appetites in your life is to lose control of your control. In chapter one, "I'm in control," we talked about control, which parallels our appetite being in control. It would be natural for us to consider the way to curb our appetite is to just change some simple rules of life. After all, I'm in control and can make it happen. We certainly can try curbing our appetite in this manner; however, it is apt to end up with failure, and we will be right back to bowing down to our appetites once again. The Bible warns us against trying this method to curb our appetites.

Man's rules will not conquer the appetites that we struggle with day in and day out. Man's rules may last for a week or two and possibly work for a few months at a time, but in the end, we find ourselves reverting back to the old passions, habits, longing, appetites, and lust of the flesh. God has a better and lasting way for us to overcome the influence of appetites in our life and our story. *"Don't handle! Don't taste! Don't touch!"? Such rules are mere human teachings about things that deteriorate as we use them. These rules may "seem wise because they require strong devotion, pious self-denial, and severe bodily discipline. But they provide no help in conquering a person's evil desires"* (Col. 2:21–23 NLT).

What you cannot accomplish in the flesh, you can accomplish in the power of Christ. Christ is the answer to your moving out of the awkward caterpillar stage of your story. No longer do you have to follow the trail of your appetites, but you can now move on to the next stage of your story line. You know you really want to fly like a butterfly. Well, of course you do, and who would not want to fly and become the beauty of the monarch butterfly? I want to encourage you with the fact that God has a plan for you, and it is to fly and become the beauty of the butterfly, as well. Because this is His plan, He has a formula for you to turn loose of the controls and to move on to the next stage of your life story.

Crucifying Our Appetites

Just as the caterpillar had to die to self in order to become a butterfly, you have to die to self and crucify the flesh, which is made up of lust, passion, desires, and appetites. *"And those who belong to Christ Jesus have crucified the sinful nature together with its passions and appetites"* (Gal. 5:24 AMP). This is the promise to those who belong to Christ. This simply applies to those who have put their faith and trust in the finished work of Jesus upon the cross and have received Jesus Christ as their personal savior. Those who belong to Christ have had their sins forgiven and have the promise of eternal life. If you have never asked God to forgive you of your sins and have asked Christ into your life, I would encourage you to take a moment right now and pray, asking for that forgiveness and asking Jesus to become your personal savior. This decision will make a tremendous change in your life. It is a defining decision and one that you will never regret you made.

Living for God's Purpose

"So that he can no longer spend the rest of his natural life living for human appetites and desires, but lives for the will and purpose of God" (1 Pet. 4:2, AMP). It really becomes a transformation in your life, which means a deep change in your life and on the pages of your

story book. Transformed from a caterpillar to a butterfly. Transformed from a flesh-controlled person to a Spirit-controlled person. Transformed from flesh-controlled to Spirit-controlled. Transformed from living for your purpose

Transformed from flesh-controlled to Spirit-controlled

in life, following the appetites of your life, to living for Christ and following His purpose for your life. When you follow God's purpose in life and you open your storybook of life and look upon the pages, you will see a drastic difference in your story from the previous pages of your life. It really becomes the difference between conforming and transforming. When we try to fix things ourselves, we usually end up conforming to manmade rules or plans. When we allow God to transform us, it will always be according to His rules or plans.

God the Transformer

The same God that can change a slinking caterpillar into a beautiful butterfly in the sky can certainly change you into something marvelous. Remember our chapter scripture, stating we are being transformed into the image of Christ by the Spirit of God. "*But we all, with unveiled face, beholding as in a mirror the glory of the Lord, are being transformed into the same image from glory to glory, just as by the Spirit of the Lord.*" Our chapter quote speaks of the exchanged life producing transformation in our lives. Life from conformed to transformed. "Transformation is a change in our lives produced by an exchange with Christ' life" (Albert Schuessler).

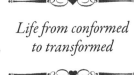

Life from conformed to transformed

The apostle Paul speaks of this exchanged life in Galatians 2:20, "*I have been crucified with Christ; it is no longer I who live, but Christ lives in me; and the life which I now live in the flesh I live by faith in the Son of God, who loved me and gave Himself for me.*" This scripture is speaking of a transformational life. The exchanged life is one that is often brought about through the darkness of brokenness. Our next chapter will bring us face to face with the caterpillar's next stage on its way to becoming a butterfly. Our next chapter will parallel chapter two, which is entitled "Who's in charge?" The caterpillar will soon learn after it is through with its eating binge that something big is going to happen in their story. It is going to be an adventure for them, but it is going to play a great role in the future of their story. We have chowed down; now it is time to take a little nap before we move on to future happenings in our life story.

Probing and Pondering, Chapter Four

WRITING YOUR STORY

- Your story line in Chapter 4: "The Caterpillar"

> *"Instead, you ought to say, 'If the Lord wills,*
> *we shall live and do this or that.'"*
> —James 4:15

EXPLORE: Study the scriptures to enhance your story line.

- *"But we all, with unveiled face, beholding as in a mirror the glory of the Lord, are being transformed into the same image from glory to glory, just as by the Spirit of the Lord."*—2 Corinthians 3:18

- *"Among whom also we all once conducted ourselves in the lusts of our flesh, fulfilling the desires of the flesh and of the mind, and were by nature children of wrath, just as the others. But God, who is rich in mercy, because of His great love with which He loved us, even when we were dead in trespasses, made us alive together with Christ by grace you have been saved.,"* — Ephesians 2:3–5

ENGAGE: developing your story line

- *"Brokenness is the pain; transformation is the gain."*—Albert Schuessler

  1. Do you believe that pain can bring gain to your spiritual life?

2. What awkward stage did you go through during your adolescence?

3. Discuss your approach when you first began to meet the opposite sex.

4. On a scale 0–10 how did you handle your lustful appetites early in life?

5. Relate to others what your relationship is with Christ at the present time.

6. Discuss your experience of the exchanged life as presented by Paul.

ENACT: applying to your story line

- *"Being transformed into the same image from glory to glory, by the Spirit."*

1. What steps can you take to leverage brokenness to your life story advantage?

2. What would a transformational change look like in your life today?

3. What sinful appetite continues in your life today that you need to curb?

4. Do you have a desire to be transformed into the beauty of a butterfly?

EMPLOY: living out your story line

- *"The butterfly displays the handiwork of God in the universe."*

    1. What can you do to help others work through their brokenness?

    2. It is important for others to see that you trust God in helping you to curb your sinful appetites.

    3. How can you leverage your brokenness to influence others?

    4. How will others see the handiwork of God when they see the transformation in your life?

Praying for ownership: Father, I ask You to help me in the times when I fear the pain in my life in order to have spiritual gain. I need You to empower me when I see my lustful appetites are getting out of hand. Lord, my desire is to experience transformation that ultimately will bring about an exchanged life. I want to exchange my life for Yours. God, I trust You when it comes to the "inside job" of brokenness in my life to produce transformation in me. Dear God, I truly want to become that beautiful butterfly in my spiritual life.

CHAPTER 5

The Cocoon

"The light shines in the darkness,
and the darkness can never extinguish it."
—John 1:5 NLT

"And do not be conformed to this world, but be transformed by the
renewing of your mind, that you may prove what is that good
and acceptable and perfect will of God."
—Romans 12:2

"Stretching your own skin like a caterpillar in a cocoon is
learning to be comfortable in your own skin."
—Albert Schuessler

I am intrigued with the study of metamorphosis and its prime example of a caterpillar transforming into a butterfly. It just seems like one of those happenings that only God can pull off. The handiwork of God is certainly seen in the metamorphose process if we are willing to take time to look at this miracle of nature. God, in His wisdom, gives us so many pictorial illustrations to help us see and understand how He works in our spiritual lives to grow us into what He would have us to become. One of the great pictures regarding our spiritual life is the transformation of a caterpillar into a butterfly. This illustration speaks volumes as to God's process for our spiritual journey.

I encourage the reader to take time with chapter four, five, and six and learn as much as you can on how God is working in your daily life. It will also be important as you are in the process of owning your story that you let your mind go back throughout your life and look at the defining moments in which transformation has changed your life in the past. Sometimes we just don't realize how God's participation in the molding and shaping of our lives is done down to the smallest detail. Our culture is awakened in excitement by the exuberance of lights, sound, and movement. We too often come to believe that God is going to be found in this exuberance as well. Due to our being accustomed to the excitement of the noise around us, we often overlook the minute workings of God. I believe that quite often, God is speaking to us and working in our lives with the little things right before our eyes that we overlook while we are seeking the big explosive things in life.

This chapter is going to point out some dark areas of life that we normally resist. We don't necessarily have a desire to enter these areas, though often we find ourselves in the darkness of a spiritual cocoon. Don't let this segment of metamorphosis scare you away from entering the cocoon stage, one of the most important steps in metamorphosis, as well as steps in your journey of life that has been defining who you are today. Though you might feel sorry for the caterpillar entering the cocoon stage, please keep in mind the positive side of his journey. In metamorphosis, he is drawing closer to his mature and glory stage of a butterfly, just as you will be drawing closer to your glory stage after you leave your spiritual cocoon. I would like to use the cocoon stage of metamorphosis to draw some very important principles about our human life story. As a believer in Christ, the cocoon stage parallels the dark times of your spiritual life journey as well.

Life and spiritual transformation are a process similar to the caterpillar entering the cocoon stage. If you recall, the caterpillar has spent a very short time on earth, consumed most of that time by his gluttonous appetite of eating. However, that stage eventually comes to an end. Once the caterpillar has eaten its fill, it will find a branch and hang upside down from that branch and go into the next stage, which is called the cocoon. The cocoon is constructed from silk. This silk comes from the spinneret organ found in the lip of the caterpillar. This organ spools out the silk while the caterpillar builds the cocoon around itself. When the liquid meets the air, it turns into a fiber, which is the silk from the caterpillar.

It is at this stage the drama begins for the caterpillar. The caterpillar finds itself inside a hard outer shell called the chrysalis, which it has created itself. Inside the chrysalis, the caterpillar has a body melt down, done by its own digestive fluids to create its new body. These fluids eventually form the body of the new creature called the butterfly. It is during this time, there is a radical transformation that changes the caterpillar into a butterfly. Yes, it is a dark stage the caterpillar must go through, but the transformation into a butterfly is well worth the dark and painful time. Yes, in your periods of transformation, it will seem very dark, and you will experience pain. However, when you reach the other side of that darkness, you will find you have been transformed into something special.

Don't Resist the Cocoon

When we experience brokenness, as described in chapters one, two, and three, it is designed to move us into the next stage I call transformation. We must be aware of the fact that no one wants to encounter the darkness and pain of transformation. This emotion sets in motion our decision to fight with all our strength not to enter this brokenness we are about to endure. We will resist brokenness with all our might. The caterpillar doesn't resist transformation. In fact, he is constantly moving toward the cocoon that ultimately results in his transformation into a butterfly. Caterpillars do not have a choice in the matter. It is going to happen to them. As the caterpillar is eating, eating, and eating, he is gradually moving into the darkness of the cocoon. They are in tune with who they are.

The caterpillar doesn't resist transformation

I do not know what your cocoon consists of or looks like or whether you have ever experienced the cocoon stage of brokenness. I don't want to minimize your darkness or your pain. You may have entered the cocoon of your life due to a health issue, a financial bankruptcy, a broken relationship ending in divorce, a failure that left you defeated, a battle with drugs and alcohol, or suffering the pain of sexual, physical, or verbal abuse. I take these experiences seriously and know the pain is very real. You see, where the caterpillar does not have a choice to enter the cocoon stage, we do have the ability to make that choice. As a matter of fact, it is more likely than not that we will resist and fight entering this painful stage. I think it is true to state that not all things are good. The things I listed previously are bad and can cause great damage to our life story. However, I also know that when we enter the cocoon stage of darkness, we are going to have to make choices.

We eventually are going to enter a painful stage of life in some manner and at some level whether we like it or not. The choices we make at this juncture of our journey are of great importance as to whether we are going to be bitter or better when we exit this parenthesis stage of life. I believe this is why we need help from people around us and from God within us in order to take a negative circumstance in our journey and turn it into a positive outcome for us to become better rather than bitter. Brokenness should make us better, rather than bitter. The following verses will help us to create this positive attitude within our minds, though our minds will be filled with negative thoughts due to our negative circumstances. At this point we need something to trigger a more positive attitude that will shed light on this darkness.

Brokenness should make us better, rather than bitter

> *And the Holy Spirit helps us in our weakness. For example, we don't know what God wants us to pray for. But the Holy Spirit prays for us with groanings that cannot be expressed in words. And the Father who knows all hearts knows what the Spirit is saying, for the Spirit pleads for us believers in harmony with God's own will. And we know that God causes everything to work together for the good of those who love God and are called according to his purpose for them. For God knew his people in advance, and he chose them to become like his Son, so that his Son would be the firstborn among many brothers and sisters.*
> (Rom. 8:26–29 NLT)

Verse 28 does not say all things are good; it says, "God causes everything to work together for good." It doesn't say God caused all the bad things to take place in our lives. Bad things happen because of the deterioration of our bodies, sin, our being in control, making bad choices, or the behavior of other people within our lives. I challenge you to muster up as much positive courage as you can to do something that seems impossible and beyond what you can carry out in your own strength. I know this attitude seems unreasonable in many of the cases you may have experienced or might experience in the future. It will take faith in God for you to believe that He can accomplish things in your story that are beyond your comprehension. Look, God is in the miracle business. He loves you and

God is in the miracle business

cares for you and is always available to minister to you in ways you cannot understand.

Think back to my comments concerning the story of Elijah in chapter 3 where God takes control of his life. We pointed out the fact that God was involved in a very intricate way in Elijah's story during his encounter with the "cocoon." Note that Elijah was worn out, beaten down, and exhausted from his cocoon experience with Jezebel. God used the angel to provide food to eat and water to drink. God continued to minister to Elijah until he had enough strength to make his journey to Mount Horeb, the mountain of God. What God was willing to do for Elijah He is willing to do for you.

> *Then as he lay and slept under a broom tree, sud-*
> *denly an angel touched him, and said to him, "Arise*
> *and eat." Then he looked, and there by his head was*
> *a cake baked on coals, and a jar of water. So, he ate*
> *and drank, and lay down again. And the angel of the*
> *Lord came back the second time, and touched him,*
> *and said, "Arise and eat, because the journey is too*
> *great for you." So, he arose and ate and drank; and he*
> *went in the strength of that food forty days and forty*
> *nights as far as Horeb, the mountain of God.*
>
> (1 Kgs 19:5–8)

In order to not resist the cocoon stage in your story, which you will be tempted to do, it is going to take a lot of faith and courage in the God of the universe for you to turn loose and give Him control of your cocoon. Your natural mindset will be to run from the cocoon, ignore the cocoon as if it is not happening, or to sweep it under the carpet and pretend that everything in your life is perfect. My challenge is for you to have a positive attitude, not in your ability, but in the ability of God. If you enter the cocoon with this attitude, it will make the cocoon stage more bearable for you. It will help you to exit the cocoon as a better person, rather than a bitter person.

Grow in the Cocoon

Having knowledge of the action taking place in the cocoon, which is out of sight to the naked eye, is important information in your understanding of what takes place in the transformation process. As you contemplate the transformation that has taken place in your story or will take place in the future, you will want to visualize how delicate and miraculous the process actually is. The process the caterpillar is going through in the cocoon to become a butterfly is very similar to the hidden action taking place in your transformational cocoon that takes place in your heart and soul, your inner person. You probably will not realize your transformation is taking place until sometime later in your story. However, you must realize the process taking place in your darkest hour is capable of changing you into a beautiful butterfly, as well. It may seem like the caterpillar is dying within the cocoon, and yet the caterpillar is transforming into a new and more beautiful life. The caterpillar is experiencing growth within the process of dying. This is a picture of our growing spiritually in the process of dying to self.

I want to expand upon my comments I made in a previous paragraph about how the dying caterpillar is growing in the cocoon. This will help you understand how important it is for you to grow in your life's cocoon. The amazing happening within the cocoon is the fact that during the caterpillar's meltdown when the cells are dying, at the same time they are creating new cells that will eventually produce the butterfly. The digestive fluids used to break down the caterpillar's body are used to produce new cells. These new cells are called imaginal cells. They congregate together as a group and come up with a plan to produce something totally different coming out of the cocoon than what went into the cocoon. A caterpillar went into the cocoon, and a butterfly came out of the cocoon.

These imaginal cells are a part of the caterpillar that holds the information that produces the butterfly. These informational cells are dormant or inactive until it is time for the butterfly to grow within the cocoon. Out of the decay and death of the crawling caterpillar inside the cocoon appears a beautiful, flying, fluttering insect called a butterfly. Incidentally, experts say that the butterfly coming out of the cocoon has the same DNA as the caterpillar going into the cocoon. This is how you visualize transformation taking place in your life by examining the metamorphoses of an insect. It is quite a phenomenal sight when you think about the process.

What important life lesson can we learn from the caterpillar dying to self in the cocoon? In Part 1 of this book, we focused on brokenness. We went into detail about the process of brokenness in our lives. Brokenness often takes place in our lives because we are in control of our affairs and our story. Putting it another way, we are self-centered and self-controlled. During brokenness, we find ourselves being transformed into something different and special.

That transformation takes place in the confines of our cocoon. In the enclosure of the cocoon, self is dealt with, and the caterpillar dies. Understanding what takes place in the cocoon of the caterpillar is very similar to what takes place in the cocoon of our lives. While in the enclosure of your life cocoon, that period where you are passing through a painful ordeal, a parenthesis, or a dark moment, you are experiencing a dying to self-transformation. The example of the caterpillar dying to his flesh in the cocoon and coming out of the cocoon totally different as a butterfly is priceless in meaning. It is a powerful example of a person dying to self in their cocoon and coming out of the cocoon as a totally different person personally and spiritually. The flesh dies in the cocoon of your life, but the spirit is energized, and you will experience a new and uplifting spiritual life. In this transformation, God is in the process of helping you to die to self, and He is actively empowering you to turn a bad situation into a situation that works together for good in your life story.

What does this good that God creates out of our bad situations look like as you come out of your dying-to-self cocoon? What will transformation produce in your life that is different than when you went into your cocoon? What will others see that's different in your life? *First,* it will give you a new direction for your life. *"Then He said to them all, "If anyone desires to come after Me, let him deny himself, and take up his cross daily, and follow Me"* (Luke 9:23). You will no longer be in control of your life, steering it into so many different and uncharted directions. You will be willing to turn from following your heart's content and start following God's heart. *Secondly,* You will become new. *"Therefore, if anyone is in Christ, he is a new creation; old things have passed away; behold, all things have become new"* (2 Cor. 5:17). You will cast aside the old things that you thought were so valuable for the new things of God. This newness of life will be fresh and pleasant and pleasing to you. *Thirdly,* You will have a changed life. *"And those who are Christ's have crucified the flesh with its passions and desires"* (Gal. 5:24). Once you die to self.

your passion and desires will change dramatically. *"Therefore, put to death your members which are on the earth: fornication, uncleanness, passion, evil desire, and covetousness, which is idolatry.."* (Col. 3:5).

The apostle Paul says if we die to ourselves, our passion and desires will no longer be focused on fornication, uncleanness, passion, evil desire, or covetousness. The longings of the flesh will be replaced with a passion for God. We will begin walking in the Spirit, rather than walking in the flesh. *Fourthly,* you will have an exchanged life. *"I have been crucified with Christ; it is no longer I who live, but Christ lives in me; and the life which I now live in the flesh I live by faith in the Son of God, who loved me and gave Himself for me"* (Gal. 2:20). You will now experience a life that is empowered by Christ. You die with Christ, you no longer live but Christ lives in you, and the life that you now live you live by faith. In the transformation sequence, you relinquish the throne of your life to the Lord Jesus Christ. He now sits on the throne of your life, and He is directing you, He is healing you, and He is empowering you to be conformed to the image of Christ. *Fifthly,* you will experience a fruitful life. *"Most assuredly, I say to you, unless a grain of wheat falls into the ground and dies, it remains alone; but if it dies, it produces much grain"* (John 12:24). If you hold a grain of wheat in your hand, it is just one grain of wheat. That grain of wheat is alone. If you plant that grain of wheat in the earth, with the help of the soil, rain, and the sun, that grain of wheat will die and will produce a sprout that in turn produces a stalk that contains a head of wheat with many grains of wheat. The original grain of wheat multiples and becomes fruitful. The same is true as you stand alone and die to self in the cocoon, so that when you exit the cocoon, your efforts will multiply, and you will live a more fruitful life. Jesus said *"I am the vine; you are the branches. He who abides in Me, and I in him, bears much fruit; for without Me you can do nothing"* (John 15:5). This verse says if we abide in Him, we will bear much fruit. It also says without Him we can do nothing.

As you see there is growth in the cocoon. Even though the caterpillar is dying in the cocoon, he is at the same time growing and transforming into a butterfly. We learned earlier that even though the transformation took place, the caterpillar and the butterfly have the same DNA. The same thing will happen to you as you die to self and come forth in Christ Jesus. You will still have the same DNA. You will have the same personality, temperament, gifts, and abilities. Inwardly, it will still be you as you were born but tweaked through the process of transformation. The point I

Grow in the cocoon

want to make is that you learn, and you grow tremendously while agonizing in your cocoon story. Grow in the cocoon.

Don't Stay in the Cocoon

When examining the cocoon, you might think after all the struggle the caterpillar is going through that when he settles down, he is nice and warm and secure inside. At this point, you might think the caterpillar is content just staying in the cocoon. Well, he might be thinking, *hey, I am protected in here I guess I will stay awhile longer*. However, if he is going to become what God intended for a caterpillar to become, he absolutely can't stay in the cocoon. The caterpillar will not reach its full potential until it becomes a butterfly and flutters and flies in the sky. Therefore, the caterpillar cannot stay in the cocoon; he must exit as a butterfly and move on with a new and more beautiful life.

The same principle is true concerning you and your cocoon battle. Once you have experienced your transformation, it is then time to move on from your cocoon trial. You cannot stay in the midst of your drama inside the cocoon. If you stay, you will never become what God has intended for you to become through your event. I have known individuals who experienced emotional pain as teenagers at the hand of their parents. Some chose to carry the pain and drama of that experience into their adult life. Instead of learning from their trial and allowing it to make them a better person and to move on with their life story, they choose to hang on to the pain and therefore become a bitter person. They allowed the situation to continue and used it in the future as their identity.

People who stayed in their cocoons were identifying with the negative when, in fact, they did not realize that they gave the person who inflicted the pain a path to continue to control their life and ultimately continue to inflict pain in their life. You see they chose to stay in the cocoon and its drama, using it to draw attention to themselves, motivated by their desire to be pitied because of what happened to them in the past. It is important that when you share your story not to draw attention to yourself and to be pitied by others. Instead, you share your story to be identified with Jesus Christ, and He becomes your identity. Christ becomes your identity because He empowered you to move out of the cocoon and to become who you are supposed to be. Now as you share your story you can say, "This is what happened to me, but I'm not that person today because Christ has carried me out of my cocoon, and I am now the person God wants me to be." You see, by staying in their cocoon, they became their own identity, and their continued pain empowered that identity. They used it to their advantage to lure people into feeling sorrow for them. Year after year, the only story they would share with other people would be how terrible they had been treated and how painful it is for them at the present time.

Yes, we want to own our story and to share our story in helping other people to see how God transformed us. We want people to know how we have become a better person from going through our event. So, sharing our story is not to draw attention to us but to draw the attention to God as to how awesome He is. We want people to see how He has transformed us so that we are conformed into being like His Son. I recall a person that had endured a painful situation early in life. They could never release this situation or the person who caused the pain. This person used the event as their identity. They did so by always bringing up their remembrance of what happened to them in the past every time they would get into a conversation with other people. That event that had happened years before was always the topic of their verbal exchange with others. They were saying, "This is who I am," instead of saying, "The pain I experienced changed me into who I am today." It would be like the butterfly saying this is who I am: a caterpillar. No, through the transformation process, you don't identify as a caterpillar; you now identify as a butterfly.

The apostle Paul describes getting out of the cocoon in the following manner in the book of Philippians. Here he shares his formula for not staying in the cocoon but exiting when transformation is complete. He is saying, "Don't stay in the cocoon." This is how you move out of the cocoon and move on with your life." This is how you can own your story before your story owns you. *"No, dear brothers and sisters, I have not achieved it, but I focus on this one thing: Forgetting the past and looking forward to what lies ahead, I press on to reach the end of the race and receive the heavenly prize for which God, through Christ Jesus, is calling us"* (Phil. 3:13–14, NLT). Paul is saying that he is forgetting the past and looking forward to what lies ahead.

Keep in mind you will never forget or get out of your mind the painful situations you have experienced in the past. There is no way to erase or eliminate what has been placed in your mind by word or by action. It is there in your mind or your subconscious mind, often buried very deep. I believe what Paul is saying to us in this scripture is to not dwell on the past, and don't let it hold you back, but focus on the future, focusing on who you can be by exiting the cocoon of your life. In other words, deal with the past, learn from it, engage it, overcome it, and own it, and then begin leveraging the past for my advantage in the future.

The cocoon stage of metamorphosis is where transformation takes place and is therefore, I believe, the most important stage of

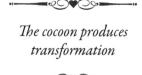

The cocoon produces transformation

our journey. The cocoon produces transformation. The caterpillar's journey begins by eating its way out of the egg and later enters the cocoon and is transformed into a beautiful butterfly as it exits the cocoon. My prayer is that you can visualize your painful circumstance in like manner as an opportunity to be transformed into a beautiful person as you exit the cocoon of your darkest hour. Visualize your past, not holding you back, but allowing it to move you forward in the rest of your journey. Visualize your new identity in Christ, the one who has rescued you and empowered you to break out of your cocoon much like a butterfly breaks out of its cocoon. Now onto the next chapter where we can experience the wings that were developed in our cocoon.

Probing and Pondering, Chapter Five

WRITING YOUR STORY

- Your story line in Chapter 5: "The Cocoon"

"Instead, you ought to say, "If the Lord wills,
we shall live and do this or that."
—James 4:15

EXPLORE: Study the scriptures to enhance your story line.

- *"And do not be conformed to this world, but be transformed by the renewing of your mind, that you may prove what is that good and acceptable and perfect will of God."* —Romans 12:2

- *"The light shines in the darkness, and the darkness can never extinguish it."* —John 1:5, NLT

ENGAGE: developing your story line

- *"Stretching your own skin like a caterpillar in a cocoon is learning to be comfortable in your own skin."* —Albert Schuessler

  1. Are you comfortable in your own skin being who you are?

  2. Discuss what it might feel like being able to not resist your cocoon.

  3. Name a time when you may have ignored, denied, or swept under the carpet a painful experience.

4.   Share with others how you grew exponentially while in your dark cocoon.

5.   What identity do you believe you portray to those around you?

6.   Discuss your experience of exiting the cocoon of your life. What has changed?

ENACT: applying to your story line

- *"Transformation is crucial to becoming who God would have you to become."*

   1.   Is there a past issue in your life you have ignored that you need to let it die?

   2.   If your pain identifies you, what steps can you take to change that identity?

   3.   Would you allow God to take your bad and turn it into good for His glory?

   4.   Are you open to God conforming you into the image of His dear Son?

EMPLOY: living out your story line

- *"Growing spiritually can be painful at times because it requires change."*

   1.   How can you use your story to let others see your identity is in Christ?

2. Are you willing to own and share your story to encourage others who find themselves amid their cocoon?

3. What type of testimony would it be if you used your past pain to draw pity to yourself?

4. Can you start the process of transformation in your life right now so others might see the mighty hand of God in your circumstance?

Praying for ownership: Father, I ask You to help me during the darkness of my cocoon stage of life. I need You to empower me to endure this stage and to help me to develop into a butterfly while struggling inside my cocoon. Lord, my desire is to experience transformation that ultimately will conform me into the image of Christ and bring glory to You. Dear God, I truly want to become that beautiful butterfly in my spiritual life. Encourage me to utilize the growth process while I am caged within the confines of the cocoon of my experience. Thank You, Jesus, for allowing me to be a human butterfly to soar to new heights in my life story.

CHAPTER 6

The Butterfly

"Why are you cast down, O my soul? And why are you disquieted within me? Hope in God; For I shall yet praise Him, The help of my countenance and my God."
—Psalm 43:5

"Why are you down in the dumps, dear soul? Why are you crying the blues? Fix my eyes on God—soon I'll be praising again. He puts a smile on my face. He's my God."
—Psalm 43:5, MSG

"But we all, with unveiled face, beholding as in a mirror the glory of the Lord, are being transformed into the same image from glory to glory, just as by the Spirit of the Lord."
—2 Corinthians 3:18

"When exiting your transformational cocoon, like a butterfly, you'll emerge as a new sight, engage with a new insight, and embark upon a new flight."
—Albert Schuessler

When we closed the cocoon chapter we left behind a dead caterpillar and a gooey mess. Even though the caterpillar was dead, its DNA was still active, and a few of its cells were still alive, forming a new body we call the butterfly. In those few weeks of living, while the caterpillar was doing what caterpillars do, crawling around like a slinky and chomping away at the leaves satisfying its humongous appetite, he was fulfilling the purpose in which he was created. The caterpillar was created to become something new and different while dying during his brokenness. It is kind of sad to leave the caterpillar behind and start a new chapter called the butterfly. What we see taking place in the cocoon of the caterpillar-to-butterfly metamorphosis is very similar to the transformation people go through in their brokenness from who they were in the past to who they are today and can be in the future. In a way, it is kind of sad to leave our old life; however, it is necessary to make the change and move on into the future.

When we go through brokenness, the process often leaves behind a gooey mess, consisting of our old lives and a dying self in the process. We might think it would be easy to give up a gooey, messy life of failure, hurt, confusion, and pain and move on. The reason it is not easy is because we do not want to give up control of our lives to God. We fear and fight the dying-to-self process. We hang on to that life with everything we have at our disposal. In other words, transformation is not a piece of cake. We fight brokenness, and in the midst of our cocoon while we are dying to self, it gets messy. Yes, dying to self gets messy! There will be times when you will be angry at yourself during your mess. You will be angry at those around you who are trying to help you dig your way out of your messy circumstance. It is quite natural at this point to be angry at God, questioning why He is allowing this pain to happen to you.

Yes, dying to self gets messy!

The struggle is real as the butterfly begins to form within the cocoon, using the imaginal cells left behind from the caterpillar in the cocoon. The soupy mess created by the caterpillar's meltdown energizes the division of the cells to form the legs, antennas, eyes, wings, and other parts of the butterfly. When it is time for the butterfly to exit the cocoon, it begins to stretch its soft wings, flex its muscles, and push with its legs to split the cocoon open. At this time, its legs slip through the crack in the cocoon, and it will gradually pull its body the rest of the way out. Whatever brokenness you have gone through or going through, you realize that when it is over, and you are exiting your cocoon that there was definitely a struggle. You have been physically, mentally, and spiritually drained, and you are weak from your experience. It takes time for you to develop and to be restored to where you can function once again as a human being.

It is at the point you are exiting your parentheses that held you back that you can begin writing your story once again. It, however, will be a defining moment and will change the direction of your life story if you choose for it to do so. You see the butterfly is weak, as well, and it takes a while for blood to flow through the wings and for the wings to dry out and develop. It takes time for the sucking mouth part called the proboscis to develop. It is used for the butterfly to feed on nectar. It takes the butterfly about twelve days to fly after it leaves the cocoon. At this point, the butterfly can do what butterflies do: fly and attract attention with their beauty. I want you to know you can experience this exhilarating moment in your story after you break loose from your painful brokenness

However, keep in mind, like the caterpillar turning into the butterfly, you are being transformed into something much greater and more beautiful than you were before you entered your cocoon. I hope and pray by now you see why I challenged you to keep a positive mind and attitude about your painful experience, knowing that

God works all things for good to those that love Him. You may not understand God's working during your mess, nor do I understand, but we must exercise our faith in Him and trust Him to develop us into that beautiful butterfly.

You Will Emerge as a New Sight

As the caterpillar and butterfly struggle within the cocoon, once you see the butterfly, you realize the struggle was well worth the effort. This transformation produces a beautiful butterfly with all its colors and characteristics that become mesmerizing as you watch them flutter and fly in your presence. The butterflies' colors are the most beautiful colors upon the earth. The Monarch butterfly is one of the topmost beautiful insects in the world. They are graced with awesome colors and will catch your eye immediately when you see one. The phenomenal color comes from two sources. The first source is pigmented colors, which are ordinary chemical pigments that absorb some wavelengths of light and reflect others. The second source is called structural colors which, of course, has to do with the structure of the butterfly's wings. The wing is covered with a great number of tiny scales and are separated from each other with air pockets. Because of the air pockets and scale movements, they flash and sparkle, highlighting the various colors. As you are watching the butterfly, you never think about the struggle it went through to get to this stage of its life, displaying its God-given beauty. The butterfly emerges from the cocoon a new sight. One can certainly see the change that has taken place from a caterpillar to a butterfly.

What does the beauty of this transformation process look like in your life? If you allow God to take your bad experience and turn it into something good, you will be wearing a new look. You will emerge as a new sight to those around you. Can I encourage you with the fact that you, too, can exit your cocoon with a new appearance? You will reflect the God-given beautiful colors of a person who has gone through the process of transformation. Think about the people who will see you in a different light. I have seen so many people who have gone through very difficult ordeals inside their life-story cocoon and emerged with a new and beautiful countenance. You will emerge from your life cocoon as a new sight to be seen.

I love the phrasing in Psalm 43:5 as paraphrased in the Message Bible. *"Why are you down in the dumps, dear soul? Why are you crying the blues? Fix my eyes on God—soon I'll be praising again. He puts a smile on my face. He's my God"* (Ps. 43:5, MSG). It states that God puts a smile on your face. In this scripture we have a man who is facing a painful cocoon experience. In other translations, it states that his soul is cast down. He is experiencing pain in the inner person. It is a hurt or a pain that is totally different than a physical pain. It is a gnawing-away pain in your inner person. You will experience it day and night as you are in the middle of your trial.

The Psalmist is experiencing the blues, depression, anguish, despair, and hopelessness. In other words, he is in a cocoon. However, he knows God is going to do something special in his story. He fixes his eyes on God. He is expecting a victory in his transformation, and soon he will be praising God once again. His parenthesis is almost over; his brokenness is coming to an end. He is going to emerge from this trial as a new sight for others to see. What changed, what made him a new sight, what has made him attractive, what made him a more beautiful person? I believe the beauty could be seen in his countenance, in his face. *"Why art thou cast down, O my soul? and why art thou disquieted within me? hope in God: for I shall yet praise him, who is the health of my countenance, and my God"* (Ps. 43:5).

You might wonder what takes place during this transformation that will cause you to look differently. It is something you

*God will heal
your countenance*

can't explain because God performs the healing you need in your inner person, your soul, your spirit—the real you. God will heal your countenance. In chapter two, I shared with you the situational depression I experienced when I was forty-five years old. I mentioned in chapter two that I would share the rest of my story in a later chapter. Here is the rest of my story that caused my countenance to reflect nothing but sadness in my life. After I tell you the rest of my story, I will share how God healed my countenance when I exited my cocoon. Two situations that happened within a year that placed me inside my life's cocoon. The two together sent me into a meltdown that took two years to recover. I share the two incidents here because they were trials in my story that I eventually had to own. When I finally owned them, they have since become a testimony to others who are facing similar trials in their life story.

The first trial took place when a member of the church I was pastoring stood up in the audience with a Bible in his hand and yelled at me, saying, "Preach the truth, brother!" Needless to say, later this led to a civil lawsuit against me. The issue was finally settled after several people in our church were deeply hurt, including me and the individual that chose to rise that day. The second trial took place within my personal family. Our son and daughter-in-law were expecting their first child and my wife and I our first grandchild in 1984. A few weeks before Rodney Cole Schuessler was born, the sonogram detected a serious issue with the growth of his brain. Rodney was born with hydrocephalus, a buildup of fluid in the cavities deep within the brain which does not allow the brain to develop in a normal way. Rodney's brain was not able to grow from the stem as it normally would. He was very much handicapped due to the lack of brain development. Rodney lived for a little over three years, passing away in June of 1987. He was a sweet boy who taught me so much about life during those three years. These two events took me into deep depression over a two-year period. The story I just shared was my most devastating life cocoon. It was not a pleasant journey, but I learned and grew from the experience and have been sharing with you in this book.

There was something different about me when I exited my cocoon. People would comment on how different I was in my appearance, as my countenance had changed. God had healed my inner person, my soul, my spirit. The inner healing was showing outwardly by the healing of my facial countenance. God's inner healing became the health of my countenance that the psalmist speaks of in Psalm 43:5. Today when I compare photographs taken of me before Rodney was born to the ones taken after God healed me, I notice a tremendous change in my appearance. In the early pictures, my countenance was without expression, with no smile on my face. My countenance had the look of the agony of defeat. In the post-cocoon pictures, I had a smile with the expression of the thrill of victory. The pictures show the transformation that took place in my life story during those two years. I emerged from the cocoon as a new sight to be seen.

You Will Engage with a New Insight

I saw a quote recently by an unknown author that said, "A lot of things broke my heart but fixed my vision." This quote speaks volumes about my experience with insight after transformation. Insight means the power of seeing into a situation more

A lot of things broke my heart but fixed my vision

deeply. It is the ability to apprehend the inner nature of a new and complicated happening in your life, to see more clearly and the understanding of a complicated situation or circumstance. Therefore, a new insight into metamorphosis is important if we are going to advance our story forward in the right direction.

We don't see our trials as they are; we see our trials as we are. When we are in control of our lives and things are going well, whether as a child or an adult, we see life pretty much like we are. Our insight might be good; however, the chances of our insight being bad is possible, as well. Once we begin the early stage of brokenness and enter the cocoon, finding ourselves during all the cocoon stages, our insight becomes somewhat foggy. We find ourselves with a dark cloud hanging over us, and our vision becomes out of focus. This causes us not to think straight in so many areas of our life. I want to list areas of my life in which my old insight was flawed. It not only affected me personally, but it carried over into other areas of my life.

My clouded insight affected every region of my surroundings at the time. My health was affected to the point that I lost weight, and I felt like I was having palpitations of the heart. I could not sleep at night, causing me to experience daily fatigue. I became very reclusive, wanting to be alone and in the dark. We had a miniature German Schnauzer dog that was a great family pet; however, during this time I could not stand being around our pet dog. I lived in fear not knowing if the people I had the privilege of pastoring had actually loved me or not. I had distanced myself from my children and their families to a certain degree. The flawed insight in my cocoon affected my relationship with my wife the most. She extended a great amount of grace to me as I was shutting her out of my life for a year. I didn't do so because I didn't love her; I shut her out because I had no real insight into my marriage due to my cocoon situation. Looking back in time, she has told me and others that all she could do was to pray for me.

What I just described took place while I was in my parentheses, or you might say, my painful cocoon. I have always identified it as experiencing brokenness. However, this brokenness does not describe me today. Why? I exited the cocoon as a different person, which catapulted me into who I am today. I experienced the butterfly phenomenon on that day. Thirty-eight years later, I still rely upon the new insight I received. I received that inward healing that changed my countenance as well as my insight into every area I have mentioned previously.

You Will Embark upon a New Flight

The caterpillar didn't have much movement, and what movement he had was very slow. The only direction he had mapped out was to the nearest milkweed. In his entire life, he spent most of his time in a small area that very well could have been within a five-foot circle. Most of the time, he might have been eating away at a few milk weeds growing side by side. The word *embark* means to begin a new course of action, launching a new path, a new direction, and a new flight. When the butterfly finally became strong, he embarked upon a new flight. The butterfly could go where the caterpillar could only dream of going. The butterfly could fly, soar high, and travel for hundreds of miles. However, to embark upon a new flight, a new life and in new scenery, the butterfly had to leave something behind. He had to leave behind the dead caterpillar, he had to leave behind the gooey mess, and he had to leave behind his old self. This leaving-behind principle is going to be important as you embark upon a new flight.

If we hang on to the brokenness and the pain it inflicts upon us, it is almost impossible to embark upon a new direction for our life after the cocoon. God's transformational goal is to forget the things of the past and to change our story into something beautiful in order to give us a new direction. Satan, on the other hand, wants you to remain fixed on the past pain of brokenness. The apostle Paul provides great insight on how to neutralize Satan's efforts and to give new direction to your life story:

> *It's not that I've already reached the goal or have already completed the course. But I run to win that which Jesus Christ has already won for me. Brothers and sisters, I can't consider myself a winner yet. This is what I do: I don't look back, I lengthen my stride, and I run straight toward the goal to win the prize that God's heavenly call offers in Christ Jesus.*
>
> (Phil. 3:12–14 GW)

Paul makes it clear that his story is not complete yet, and he is still writing it. He says I can't consider myself a winner yet. His next statement is key to your success of becoming a winner in life after the pain of your brokenness, saying, "I don't look back." He teaches us to leverage the pain of brokenness by lengthening our stride forward and don't look back but run straight toward the goal, the prize of life in Jesus Christ.

As mentioned before, whatever your painful experience has been in the past, it no doubt will always be in your mind. There is no way to erase it from your mind. However, there is a way to limit its power of control over you in the future. That power can be neutralized the same way Satan's fixation power can be neutralized in tempting you to stay in the cocoon. I want to reiterate again that

I do not want to minimize the pain you have suffered. Through the pages of this book, I simply want to help you to work past that pain and find new direction for your life story. More importantly I encourage you to see God's plan for you to have the courage for you to take the steps needed to lengthen your stride forward.

I found for me to embark upon a new flight, I had to work through the transformation of my mind. I had to begin thinking like Jesus thinks. *"Let this mind be in you, which was also in Christ Jesus "*(Phil. 2:5). *First,* I had to come to an understanding of what brokenness really was and what it looked like. It was very difficult for me to find the answers to my questions. My pastor friends at that time had little knowledge as to the principle of brokenness. It seemed like I was in the wilderness, and somehow I stumbled upon a book that had a chapter in it about brokenness. I finally found some answers to my questions and learned a great deal about the brokenness that I am sharing with you in this book. *Secondly,* I had to own the pain of brokenness in my story. I didn't want to admit that I was experiencing deep depression. As a man, it seemed like a weak position to admit that I did not have control of my life. What would people think about me being a pastor who was not able to apply the scriptures about worry to my own life? *Thirdly,* I had to own my story. There came a day when I simply said that is what happened to me, and that is who I am, thus owning my story. From that point on my life, I embarked upon a new direction. That is when God was able to heal my countenance. It has made a difference in all my relationships with family and friends. It has made a difference in my outlook upon life. I have a more positive attitude about life itself. I see the world more like it is instead of how I am, and most importantly it has deepened my relationship with the Lord Jesus Christ.

Right now, as you read this chapter, it could be a defining moment in your life story. I cannot think of a more appropriate time for you to pray and ask God to provide strength to you in order to own your story. Maybe you are someone reading this chapter, and you are saying, "I am in transition at the present time." Possibly you are an individual reading this book and saying, "I know exactly what you are writing about." You are now the one that can share your story because sometime in the past you owned your story.

I want to share with you my life verses that I have adopted into my mind and into the heart of my life story since exiting from my cocoon and finding myself on a new flight. The following verses are the ones that have lifted me to new heights in my life in general and my spiritual life more specifically.

> *That He would grant you, according to the riches of His glory, to be strengthened with might through His Spirit in the inner man, that Christ may dwell in your hearts through faith; that you, being rooted and grounded in love, may be able to comprehend with all the saints what is the width and length and depth and height— to know the love of Christ which passes knowledge; that you may be filled with all the fullness of God. Now to Him who is able to do exceedingly abundantly above all that we ask or think, according to the power that works in us, to Him be glory in the church by Christ Jesus to all generations, forever and ever. Amen.* (Eph 3:16–21)

I can embark upon a new direction because I have a new strength. New strength provides new direction. It is an inner strength that I never had before in my entire life. I work out at the gym a couple of times a week to tone up and to build up my muscle strength. I think it is important to exercise our bodies. I never once considered exercising my inner person to give me strength to deal with the brokenness I was experiencing. Now I see the importance of allowing the Holy Spirit to build my inner wings to support the flight I am taking today. Notice in verse 20, Paul says that God can do abundantly above all that we could ask or even think, according to the power He works in us. It is that power to carry us

New strength provides new direction

through the cocoon experience and to heal our countenance. It is that power to take our bad experiences and work them for good in our lives, even though we do not understand how He accomplishes that feat.

The picture I would like to leave with you as I conclude this chapter is God dealing with your gooey mess inside your cocoon. Visualize that mess placed within His hands and He is taking each piece of the puzzle of your story placing it in the slot where it belongs. He is working your mess within His hands to produce good in your life.

Own your story today by putting your past behind you and stretching your life forward with a smile on your face. Allow God to bring healing to your countenance right now. Only when we say, "Yes, this is who I am, this is my story, I own this story, and I am moving on in a new direction" can we truly find this healing. Happy flight; flutter away for all it's worth.

Probing and Pondering, Chapter Six

WRITING YOUR STORY

- Your story line in Chapter 6: "The Butterfly"

"Instead, you ought to say, 'If the Lord wills,
we shall live and do this or that.'"
—James 4:15

EXPLORE: Study the scripture to enhance your story line.

- *"Why are you cast down, O my soul? And why are you disquieted within me? Hope in God; For I shall yet praise Him, The help of my countenance and my God."* —Psalm 43:5

- *"Why are you down in the dumps, dear soul? Why are you crying the blues? Fix my eyes on God—soon I'll be praising again. He puts a smile on my face. He's my God."* —Psalm 43:5, MSG

- *"But we all, with unveiled face, beholding as in a mirror the glory of the Lord, are being transformed into the same image from glory to glory, just as by the Spirit of the Lord."* —2 Corinthians 3:18

ENGAGE: developing your story line

- *"Why are you down in the dumps, dear soul? Why are you crying the blues?*

   1. Has there been a time when your soul has been down in the dumps?

2. Discuss the difference between an outward beauty and inward beauty.

3. Discuss your personal insight of a past cocoon experience you've had.

4. Discuss your present-day insight of that same experience after exiting that cocoon as a butterfly.

5. Discuss how God is or has worked in your life, stretching you forward in your story.

6. Can you visualize what your gooey mess can become in the hands of God?

ENACT: applying to your story line

- *Fix my eyes on God—soon I'll be praising again. He puts a smile on my face. He's my God."*

  1. What steps can you take to keep your past pain from influencing your present life direction?

  2. What would you need to release today for God to be in control of your gooey mess?

  3. Are you courageous enough to own your story today?

  4. Will you allow the Holy Spirit to strengthen your inner wings for flight?

EMPLOY: living out your story line

- *"When exiting your transformational cocoon, like a butterfly, you'll emerge as a new sight, engage with a new insight and embark upon a new flight."* —Albert Schuessler

1. It is important that you share your new beauty with others for them to see the glory of God

2. Share with others how owning your story has released you from your past pain.

3. Share your new spiritual insight with those who are presently struggling with issues inside their cocoon.

4. Advance the glory of God by sharing your inner beauty and strength to those around you.

Praying for ownership: Father, I am out of the cocoon, and I am a new and beautiful person. I want to leverage this new beauty and to allow my life to be used by You to help others find healing for their lives. Lord, my desire is to experience full transformation that ultimately will conform me into the image of Christ and bring glory to You. Dear God, thank You for the new sight that I have become and the new insight You have given me and the new flight and direction I have embarked upon. Stretch me to fly like a butterfly should fly.

PART 3

The Flexibility of Transparency

A h, transparency. Who doesn't like being exposed for who they are? Who doesn't relish the opportunity to open their lives up and let the world see them as they really are and not what they project who they think they are? One of the objectives of this book is for you to see the positive progression of God's working in your life journey. So far in describing your journey with Him, it seems more negative than positive. I believe as you move through Part 3, you will be able to see the positive outcome He has for your journey. In this section of the book, I am going to focus on the influence of transparency that is developed in our lives through the experience of brokenness and transformation. Transparency in our lives is less about us and more about God's work within our lives and can be defined as a tangible item, such as glass, that allows rays of light to transmit through its substance so that whatever is located on the back side can be clearly seen. In other words, an item is transparent if you can see right through it.

What does this transparency involve in a person's life? It simply means that you allow others to see you as you are and that you have nothing to hide. Allowing people to see through you means that you will become vulnerable, open, and flexible. It will transform you from being rigid and judgmental toward others into someone that will be more flexible in all your relationships. When you reach the point in your life of owning your story, you will become greatly influential to others because you have reached the point of transparency.

It is quite common for us to sweep under the carpet and hide embarrassing experiences of the past. Most of us have things in the past that we are ashamed of, and we hide them in the dark room of our hearts as long as we can. When we hide our embarrassing experiences, we become chained to them and find ourselves in bondage. Transformation is like a pair of chain cutters, slicing through a chain link fence to set us free. This freedom we experience allows us to unlock the dark room and sets us free to become honest, true, and transparent. Enjoy the transparent stage of your life journey.

CHAPTER 7

Humility

"Humble yourselves in the sight of the Lord, and He will lift you up."
—James 4:10

"Pride goes before destruction, And a haughty spirit before a fall."
—Proverbs 16:18

"Humility is the ladder that will lift you to
new heights in your life journey."
—Albert Schuessler

"Appreciate God lifting you up in humility
in order to keep you from falling in pride."
—Albert Schuessler

The minute we have escaped the messy cocoon stage of life and are flying like a butterfly, we will soon face a new set of opportunities. However, the new opportunities will be different than the ones we just finished. The new opportunities are not as painful as the previous ones were, but nevertheless, there is a certain amount of fear that comes along with them. Entering the

*Transparency opens
the door for us to
be examined*

transparency stage of your life journey brings with it several things we are not comfortable with. It is important to realize that, with the new opportunities, you'll not experience pain, but you may experience discomfort. Transparency opens the door for us to be examined. Our family and friends will be examining our motives as to why we have acted a certain way. Transparency sees right through us and exposes our past failures and our present weaknesses. Transparency allows others to see directly into your life and to read you like an open book. That's not all bad because it is your book, and you have been going through the process of owning your book. Don't fear this transparency segment of your life. When you allow it to happen, it will set you free of all your fears you have about allowing people to read your life story.

Being humble is something most of us fear. We fear the process by which humility takes place in our lives, usually through brokenness. We also fear the fact that in our culture, humility is often seen as a weakness in a person's life. Very seldom do we ever imagine or is it ever taught that humility is actually the means by which one rises to the pinnacle of life. At this point of your journey, as you think about humility, it will take your mind back to chapter one, titled "I'm in Control." You can see how far you have come in your journey of life. How different life can be when comparing a life of pride to one of humility where you allow God to be in control. Chapter one pictured a life filled with pride. However, we have traveled a long way down the road from chapter one. A lot has gone under the bridge of life, as we have experienced and learned volumes in the journey, and the cocoon stage has produced its humility. So, it isn't going to hurt, but it will be a little uncomfortable.

An Inward Humility

Humility helps us to find who we really are in the inward person. Humility is a point of reference in marking our life identification. Who you believe you are is paramount in owning your story. If you cannot pinpoint who you are then you will never feel comfortable in your own skin. The Apostle Paul in the book of Romans gives us some good advice in identifying who God expects us to be. *"For I say, through the grace given to me, to everyone who is among you, not to think of himself more highly than he ought to think, but to think soberly, as God has dealt to each one a measure of faith."* (Rom. 12:3) Pride is found in the mind. Pride is in our thinking process and once there it is a spark of pride in our thinking, it will explode into a mushroom of arrogance. In Romans 12:3, it says *"not to think of himself more highly than he ought to think"* in other words don't be vain or come off in an arrogant manner. Paul continues with using the word soberly. Soberly means being of sound mind or being in the right mind using moderation and self-restraint about yourself. If one is in their right mind they will not think of themselves as someone overly important.

When people see your transparency, they will see someone in their right mind who isn't filled with arrogance. The way one gets to this point of humility is to draw near to God. The process of drawing near to God is through brokenness and transformation. James alludes to this process in James 4:6–10, where he speaks of drawing near to God:

> *But He gives more grace. Therefore, He says: "God resists the proud, But gives grace to the humble." Therefore, submit to God. Resist the devil and he will flee from you. Draw near to God and He will*

draw near to you. Cleanse your hands, you sinners; and purify your hearts, you double-minded. Lament and mourn and weep! Let your laughter be turned to mourning and your joy to gloom. Humble yourselves in the sight of the Lord, and He will lift you up."

God resists the proud, the one appearing above others, but He gives grace to the one who is humble, the one of low degree. Make no mistake; when God says something to us through His Word, you can take it to mean exactly what it says.

You might look at transparency and the humility that goes along with it and say, "This is a losing proposition." Maybe you are thinking, *I don't want to be identified as a loser.* Possibly you are thinking that only the proud and arrogant people seem to be winners in life. I know our culture identifies the humble as weak and the proud as strong. The world would say the weak are losers and the proud are winners. Let's see what the psalmist has to say about the losers and winners in life. *"For the Lord delights in his people; he crowns the humble with victory"* (Ps. 149:4, NLT). Notice the opposite is true; God crowns the humble with victory. Isn't this awesome to think about? Inner humility identifies you as being a winner. You are the one that receives the victory, not the proud.

Inner humility identifies you as being a winner

An Outward Humility

We live in a narcissistic culture, with a philosophy that everybody is in it for themselves. That philosophy is "It's not about you; it's all about me." The culture's attitude is "I want to be first in line;

serve me first or give me a discount because I deserve it." When you witness road rage on the highway, it is usually because someone thought they were more important than the person in the other vehicle. The one in a rage thinks the other person should move over and let them pass them because they are more important. The driver that is on the bumper of another vehicle, while going at a high rate of speed on the major highway is saying, "Move over. I am more important than you." We see it in churches where ethics is put aside by one church willing to take people from another church to grow their church. It is seen in a church setting where we might think our God-given spiritual gift is more important than someone else's gift. You often see narcissism in our culture when the rich and famous people think they are above the law or above the average people in our society. It is quite natural for us to put our interests first.

Once we experience the inward humility of brokenness and become more transparent, we automatically become more influential within the relationships around us. Of course, the reason for being more influential is that we are not so fixated on ourselves but now place our fixation on other people. Many of the people you humble yourself to are down and out. In other words, we begin to see the value in people around us. Therefore, our humility is more focused outward rather than inward. Before our brokenness, we placed all our value totally upon ourselves in an attitude of pride and conceit. But now, instead of being a legend in our own minds, we now see the worth in our family members and friends.

We might be a little surprised at this scenario, but this is God's plan for the believer. Notice the apostle Paul's admonition in the following scripture. *"Let nothing be done through selfish ambition or conceit, but in lowliness of mind let each esteem others better than himself. Let each of you look out not only for his own interests, but also for the interests of others"* (Phil. 2:3–4). Notice how Paul challenges us to take our attention off ourselves and place it on others around us. Selfish ambition and conceit are not a way of life for the believer. We are to esteem or value others better than ourselves. There will always be a tension between your interest and the interest of others.

> *There will always be a tension between your interest and the interest of others*

Humility values God's plan in placing value on others, rather than ourselves. Paul wrote to the believers in Rome about honoring one another: *"Love one another with brotherly affection. Outdo one another in showing honor"* (Rom. 12:10, ESV). Tell me how in the world is it possible to outdo another person in honoring them over ourselves. The only way is through being transparent with the humility that brokenness and transformation has produced in our lives. You will give a lot of attention to what you value. If you value others highly, then you will give them a lot of attention.

However, Paul is not at all saying that you should not have self-value or self-worth of who you are. Paul simply says to not think of yourself more highly than you ought but to think soberly or in the right mind with moderation and self-restraint about yourself. *"For I say, through the grace given to me, to everyone who is among you, not to think of himself more highly than he ought to think, but to think soberly, as God has dealt to each one a measure of faith"* (Rom. 12:3). For instance, the Bible says you are to love your neighbor as yourself. You could never love your neighbor if you did not have love for who you are. In the Gospel of Mark we read, *"For what will it profit a man if he gains the whole world, and loses his own soul? Or what will a man give in exchange for his soul?"* You could not value others if you did not have value for yourself. Your inner person, your soul, is so valuable that you have absolutely nothing that you could exchange in value for who you are. Don't lose sense of your value; just keep it in check, and don't let it stimulate pride within your mind.

Upward Humility

In our culture, it is etched into our minds at an early age that we must climb the ladder of success. In other words, getting on the ladder is the only way up. Never look back or never look down because that will result in failure. Much of the world follows this pattern. That is why it is often called a "dog-eat-dog world." This phrase is used to describe a world in which people will do anything to become successful even if what they do will hurt you. So, in our society, you will see, and experience people walking all over other people to get ahead and become successful. I believe the biblical plan is just the opposite of the world pattern. This is not a theological statement, but in my mind God uses reverse psychology when it comes to being successful in life. The Bible makes it clear that the way up is first down. Jesus Christ is the prime example of this biblical principle. At this point, let's first look at the biblical principle, and then we'll examine the great example Jesus has left us on being lifted up.

First, as you can clearly see in chapter 4 of the book of James that he lays out God's formula for becoming a success in life. It is what I call upward humility as being the way of success. Humility is one of the most important aspects of transparency. Ultimately brokenness and transformation will lift you up to transparency through humility. Take a moment to search this scripture to have a greater understanding of the value of humility:

> *But He gives more grace. Therefore, He says: "God resists the proud, But gives grace to the humble."*

Therefore, submit to God. Resist the devil and he will flee from you. Draw near to God and He will draw near to you. Cleanse your hands, you sinners; and purify your hearts, you double-minded. Lament and mourn and weep! Let your laughter be turned to mourning and your joy to gloom. Humble yourselves in the sight of the Lord, and He will lift you up.

(James 4: 6–10)

Notice that God resists the proud and gives grace to the humble. Do you see how important it is to God that we are humble? However, the dilemma comes when, in our natural state, we are filled with pride. We may say we are humble, but just saying we are humble with no evidence of humility is an indication that it is a false humility. We fight humility because it deflates our pride. A person filled with pride will find it difficult to be transparent and talk about their fears, failures, and weaknesses.

In verse 10, James tells us to humble ourselves in the sight of the Lord, and He will lift us up. This is what I call your upward humility. The journey to humble yourself comes through the brokenness and transformation of your painful situation in life. Humility is a must if we are going to own our stories before they own us. To be humble means that you are willing to accept and own your failures and to be transparent enough to share them with other people. Make no mistake about it; in the Gospel of Luke, he makes it clear in recording a dialogue Jesus was having with the Pharisees and rulers that humility is essential in the kingdom of God. In the following verses you see Jesus's discourse with individuals that are filled with pride. One identification mark of a Pharisee was their attitude of pride. Jesus addresses that attitude by teaching them the importance of humility. Take note of what He says in the parable.

So He told a parable to those who were invited, when He noted how they chose the best places, saying to them: "When you are invited by anyone to a wedding feast, do not sit down in the best place, lest one more honorable than you be invited by him; and he who invited you and him come and say to you, 'Give place to this man,' and then you begin with shame to take the lowest place. But when you are invited, go and sit down in the lowest place, so that when he who invited you comes he may say to you, 'Friend, go up higher.' Then you will have glory in the presence of those who sit at the table with you. For whoever exalts himself will be humbled, and he who humbles himself will be exalted." (Luke 14:7-11)

Jesus makes it clear if we want to be noticed and if we want to have the most favored position above those who are lower, then we are exalting ourselves. In other words, we are thinking too highly of ourselves and thinking of our interest first and not the interest of other people. Notice in our scripture the power of transparency. When you experience the humility of transparency, then Jesus said you will be exalted. I know this does not sound reasonable, but I can assure you, it sounds biblical.

Secondly, Jesus gives us a great example of what this humility journey looks like in His own life story: *Let this mind be in you which was also in Christ Jesus, **who**, being in the form of God, did not consider it robbery to be equal with God, but made Himself of no reputation, taking the form of a bondservant, and coming in the likeness of men. And being found in appearance as a man, He humbled Himself and became obedient to the point of death, even the death of the cross. Therefore God also has highly exalted Him and given Him* *the name which is above every name, **that** at the name of Jesus every knee should bow, of those in heaven, and of those on earth, and of those under the earth.* (Phil. 2:5–10) Knowing what Jesus went through in His life helps you to realize the value of your journey to this point where you have been humbled, which consequently produced transparency in your life. The value is that you have the mind of Christ, *"For who has known the mind of the Lord that he may instruct Him?" But we have the mind of Christ"* (1 Cor. 2:16), and He wants your mind to be like His mind that was filled with humility. Jesus was not arrogant about the fact that He was God. If anyone had a right to be arrogant and to go around bragging about the fact that He was God, it would be Jesus. He chose just the opposite and became in the likeness of men. His journey was from being God to being in the likeness of men, from being Deity to being humanity. He humbled himself and became obedient even unto death.

Philippians 2:9–10 tells us that God honored Jesus's debasing Himself by highly exalting Him and giving Him a name, which is above every name. Paul continues the exaltation by saying *"that at the name of Jesus every knee should bow."* Keep in mind that Jesus is God, and God isn't going to give you a name above all names so that everyone will bow down to you. By using Jesus's example, I simply want to direct you to the principle that humility will give you a powerful life at a new level. It is a new level of satisfaction, tranquility, serving, peace, openness, fearlessness, and magnetism drawing hurting people to you. God will use your life in a new way that will be pleasing to Him and a blessing to you. Being lifted by God through humility will be an ointment to the wounds you have had in the past.

Humility will give you a powerful life at a new level

Why All the Fuss About Humility?

The question then is why all the fuss about humility in our journey? Why must we suffer the pain along the way in becoming humble? Isn't there another way in which we can experience humility? Is there not another avenue that we can travel to become transparent? In order to escape pain, couldn't we just live with pride and continue on writing our story? What difference does it really make whether we are filled with pride or whether we are humble? The fact of the matter is we can choose to ignore God's plan and live our lives filled with arrogance and pride and let our story record that choice.

To answer the questions within our minds, we must go back to the admonition of letting our minds be like the mind of Christ Jesus. In other words, we are to think like Jesus thinks. Jesus's thoughts were totally about being humble. "

> *Do not love the world or the things in the world. If anyone loves the world, the love of the Father is not in him. For all that is in the world—the lust of the flesh, the lust of the eyes, and the pride of life—is not of the Father but is of the world. And the world is passing away, and the lust of it; but he who does the will of God abides forever.* (1 John 2:15–17)

John answers our question concerning pride when he lists three things that tempt us in life: the lust of the flesh, the lust of the eyes, and the pride of life. The pride of life is the culprit that causes us so much pain. We are tempted with pride every day. The reason Jesus is our example of humility is that He experienced the pride issue the same as you experience the pride issue. After Jesus was baptized,

He was led by the Spirit into the wilderness. Matthew records in his gospel an encounter that Jesus had with Satan. Notice in the following scripture the weapons of temptation Satan used against Jesus were the same ones that John speaks of in his letter. Notice the discourse between Jesus and Satan in Matthew's gospel:

> *Then Jesus was led up by the Spirit into the wilderness to be tempted by the devil. And when He had fasted forty days and forty nights, afterward He was hungry. Now when the tempter came to Him, he said, "If You are the Son of God, command that these stones become bread." But He answered and said, "It is written, 'Man shall not live by bread alone, but by every word that proceeds from the mouth of God.' 'Then the devil took Him up into the holy city, set Him on the pinnacle of the temple, **and** said to Him, "If You are the Son of God, throw Yourself down. For it is written: 'He shall give His angels charge over you,' and, 'In their hands they shall bear you up, lest you dash your foot against a stone.' "Jesus said to him, "It is written again, 'You shall not tempt the Lord your God.' " Again, the devil took Him up on an exceedingly high mountain, and showed Him all the kingdoms of the world and their glory. And he said to Him, "All these things I will give You if You will fall down and worship me." Then Jesus said to him, "Away with you, Satan! For it is written, 'You shall worship the Lord your God, and Him only you shall serve.'" Then the devil left Him, and behold, angels came and ministered to Him.* (Matt. 4:1–11)

Satan took Jesus to a mountaintop and showed Him all the kingdoms of the world and said, "I will give you all these kingdoms if you will bow down and worship me." If these kingdoms were offered to you like they were offered to Jesus, I guarantee you that the pride of life would swell up in you immediately. In answering the question why, this is just one of the reasons that pride must be dealt with. Jesus wanted nothing to do with anything that would stimulate pride in His life. He warns us about pride throughout the scriptures because He does not want us to fall for the glory offered us by pride. Actually, the issue of pride goes all the way back to Adam and Eve when they were tempted in the Garden of Eden:

> *Now the serpent was more cunning than any beast of the field which the Lord God had made. And he said to the woman, "Has God indeed said, 'You shall not eat of every tree of the garden'?" And the woman said to the serpent, "We may eat the fruit of the trees of the garden; but of the fruit of the tree, which is in the midst of the garden, God has said, 'You shall not eat it, nor shall you touch it, lest you die.' Then the serpent said to the woman, "You will not surely die. For God knows that in the day you eat of it your eyes will be opened, and you will be like God, knowing good and evil." So, when the woman saw that the tree was good for food, that it was pleasant to the eyes, and a tree desirable to make one wise, she took of its fruit and ate. She also gave to her husband with her, and he ate.* (Gen. 3:1–6)

In verse 6, Eve saw that the fruit was from a tree that would make her wise and that she would now have the knowledge of good and evil. She fell for the same bait that was placed before Jesus. Unlike Jesus, however, she nibbled away until she bit the bait and caused sin to enter humanity. According to the proverbs: *"Pride goes before destruction, And a haughty spirit before a fall" (Prov. 16:18).* The word *haughty* means arrogant. The brokenness and transformation we experience is a means in which God uses to lead us away from pride and arrogance and to replace it with transparency.

I encourage you to claim your transparency and to assimilate it into your story. Experience the joy of exposing your life to others for them to see deep into who you have become. Let them see your butterfly experience. You have owned your failures and weaknesses in your story, and now you are free to share them with others through your humility. Appreciate God lifting you up in humility to keep you from falling in pride.

Probing and Pondering, Chapter Seven

WRITING YOUR STORY

- Your story line in Chapter 7: "Humility"

> *"Instead, you ought to say, 'If the Lord wills,*
> *we shall live and do this or that.'"*
> —James 4:15

EXPLORE: Study the scriptures to enhance your story line.

- *"Humble yourselves in the sight of the Lord, and He will lift you up."* —James 4:10

- *"Pride goes before destruction, And a haughty spirit before a fall."* —Proverbs 16:18

ENGAGE: developing your story line

- "Humility is the ladder that will lift you to new heights in your life journey" —Albert Schuessler

  1. Has arrogance ever been an issue in your life?

  2. Assuming you are out of your cocoon, share how that experience has humbled you.

  3. Discuss how you think God can use humility to lift you up to new heights in your life.

  4. Discuss if you think the inward humility of transformation produces losers or winners.

5. Discuss some characteristics that would indicate that you are comfortable in your own skin.

6. Do you appreciate it when others are transparent with you? Why?

ENACT: applying to your story line

- "Appreciate God lifting you up in humility in order to keep you from falling in pride." —Albert Schuessler

   1. What steps can you take to assure that you have a correct identification of who you are?

   2. Pride is powerful; what steps might you take in overcoming pride in your life/

   3. How can you guard against Satan tempting you with the weapon of pride?

EMPLOY: living out your story line

- *"Humble yourselves in the sight of the Lord, and He will lift you up."*

   1. Be challenged to share your failures and weaknesses in humility.

   2. Sharing your humility through transparency can help others not to fall in pride.

   3. Be humble enough to think of others' interests instead of your own interest.

Praying for ownership: Father, transparency can be uncomfortable at times. Sharing my weaknesses and failures is not easy, and I need Your power to do so. I pray You will empower me to think of what others are experiencing rather than being focused on my own interest. Father, I don't want to be someone else; I just want to be me. Lord, help me to come to the point that I can be comfortable in my own skin. Father, I ask You to challenge me in making changes in my life. Encourage me to come alongside others when their lives need my transparency.

CHAPTER 8

Vulnerability

*Oh, dear Corinthian friends! We have spoken honestly with you, and
our hearts are open to you. There is no lack of love on our part, but
you have withheld your love from us. I am asking you to respond as if
you were my own children. Open your hearts to us!*
—2 Corinthians 6:11–13, NLT

*And when Jesus was in Bethany at the house of Simon the leper, a
woman came to Him having an alabaster flask of very costly fragrant
oil, and she poured it on His head as He sat at the table. But when
His disciples saw it, they were indignant, saying, "Why this waste?
For this fragrant oil might have been sold for much and given to the
poor. But when Jesus was aware of it, He said to them, "Why do you
trouble the woman? For she has done a good work for Me. For you
have the poor with you always, but Me you do not have always.*
—Matthew 26:6–11

Bear one another's burdens, and so fulfill the law of Christ.
—Galatians 6:2

"Exposing your imperfections will make you vulnerable,
which in turn will make you accessible"
—Albert Schuessler

"Exchanging your weakness for God's strength is
experienced in your vulnerability"
—Albert Schuessler

O nce transformation is processed in your life story and you
take on the role of being transparent, you will experience
the exposure of your soul. When you are at peace with transparency,
which may take a while, you will then find yourself in the position
of vulnerability. The more transparent you become, the more you
will find yourself letting your protective guard down and becoming
more vulnerable. What does this vulnerability look like in your life?
It means you are open to criticism, susceptible to emotional injury,
and exposed to personal attack. It means you will be exposed to
physical and emotional hurt. Only individuals that are willing to
become transparent will experience what it is like to be satisfied in
their own skin. Vulnerability is just one more step in the process of
owning your story before your story owns you.

I have often thought how vulnerable God became when Jesus,
who is God, was conceived and dwelling in His mother's womb.
You may have read the accounts in the gospels recording His conception, birth, life, death, and resurrection Think about Jesus being
held in the fragile hands of Mary. Visualize His mother hugging and
squeezing Him. I marvel when I think about His mother placing
Him on her shoulder and burping Him. Yes, little babies need to
have their diapers changed quite often. She could have been careless
and hurt Him by dropping Him. Can you see Him in swaddling
clothes lying in the manger, with animals all around Him? Can you
perceive Him running through the streets of the city where He lived?

He was also vulnerable throughout the Old Testament as well.
Satan was trying frantically to destroy the lineage in which He was
to be born. You read about Herod, the Chief Priest, the Sanhedrin,

Pharisees, and people in the street crying "crucify Him." Even though Jesus may have seemed to be at His weakest point, He really was at His strongest point throughout His birth and life. In His vulnerability, God was not going to allow anything to happen to Jesus, much like God would not allow anything to happen to Moses in the Old Testament when His mother put him in the basket to float down the Nile River. Moses was well protected by the hands of God. This vulnerability of Jesus provides for you an important aspect of what vulnerability really looks like in one's life.

When You Are Weak, You Become Strong

It does not seem possible that you could be strong at your weakest point. This statement might seem absurd in a society where it is promoted that the strong are the ones who always win. No doubt, the strong do win in many areas of life, and it is certainly true in most sporting events. In Darwin's philosophy of evolution, it is stated the "survival of the fittest." I suppose in the animal world, this would be the case. However, in the game of life, the scriptures present a different picture of swtrength. Scripture points out vulnerability produces your weakest point but provides your strongest platform.

Vulnerability produces your weakest point but provides your strongest platform

In 2 Corinthians, chapter 12, Paul speaks of God giving him a thorn in the flesh to prevent him from becoming proud of what He had seen in his third-heaven experience. In other words, God wanted Paul to be humble as we talked about in chapter 7. Paul pleaded with God three times to remove this thorn in the flesh. But notice God said to Paul, "My grace is sufficient" and then He declares "my strength is made perfect in weakness." After hearing what God said, Paul then came to the conclusion and stated, "For when I am weak, then I am strong." (II Cor. 12:8-10) In reading the following verses you can see how your story will be strengthened in the moments of your vulnerability.

> *Concerning this thing I pleaded with the Lord three times that it might depart from me. And He said to me, "My grace is sufficient for you, for My strength is made perfect in weakness." Therefore, most gladly I will rather boast in my infirmities, that the power of Christ may rest upon me. Therefore, I take pleasure in infirmities, in reproaches, in needs, in persecutions, in distresses, for Christ's sake. For when I am weak, then I am strong.*

We learn that vulnerability helps us to recognize our dependence upon God and His strength. When we are transparent, everyone has the opportunity to look inside and examine our life and our soul. They will see the core of your life, both physically and emotionally. Because our life is open to others, it would seem that we would be in a state of weakness. However, for us to be transparent, we have had to experience the power of God in our journey. It is natural for humans to believe that the stronger we are, the greater chance we have to win in life. It is true that in the book of Joshua, chapter 1, God encourages Joshua to be strong and of good courage. However, God reminds Joshua that He would be with them. They were to be strong and of good courage in God's power and strength.

There is always the need in our lives to be strengthened by the Holy Spirit of God. *"That He would grant you, according to the riches of His glory, to be strengthened with might through His Spirit in the inner man"* (Eph. 3:16). Brokenness and transformation take place in the inner man, and therefore, transparency springs forth like an artesian well from your inner person. We may build our bodies at the gym to become strong physically, but make no mistake about it, the only way we become strong in our spiritual life is through the power of the Holy spirit. Our inner strength is developed by the Holy Spirit.

Our inner strength is developed by the Holy Spirit

Once you can see the process of becoming vulnerable through transparency, you will see the benefit of God's power upon your life in exchange for your weakness. It is at this point of weakness and becoming vulnerable, that your life finds real meaning, and you become extremely effective and influential in ministering to those who are having difficulty with their life journey. Your new strength will help you climb the walls standing before you that are holding you back from owning your story. Your vulnerability is a segment of owning your story before your story owns you.

Your Vulnerability Is Your Greatest Strength

Once you become transparent, you are apt to step out and share with others a few of your life experiences that will make you vulnerable with your friends. Some of the things I am listing at this point would certainly make the super pious people in the church turn their heads in disgust. Here are a few explosive things you might decide to release from your heart. For instance, you might admit that you do not have all the answers to life. This will expose you and cause many to think you are a phony. Owning up to the fact that you have made mistakes in the past and willing to share them will make you a moving target for others to take a potshot at you. Sharing that you were a mess in your cocoon stage of life will shock a few people. Acknowledging your weaknesses will draw mockery from certain people. If you expose your soul in these areas you certainly will become vulnerable in the sphere of your influence.

Another area a transparent person might become vulnerable is stepping out to minister to difficult people and high-maintenance individuals. For instance, you might reach out and minister to hurting people that you normally would not give the time of day to. So much ministering to people is done inside the safety of a church building. Certainly, there is always going to be several people experiencing pain in the church. This ministry is very much needed in our churches in America and around the world. The Bible mentions many ways in which we are to minister to one another in the church. I have noticed that people of transparency often make their way outside the church walls to minister to people as well.

Looking around us we can readily see the need for ministry in our prisons. Streets in the big cities often are filled with homeless people with no place to live. Mental health has become a big issue in our cluttered and painful society. The church, in many cases, has buried its head in the sand, not wanting to spend the time or money to deal with those in mental need. Why do we neglect those with mental health issues? I believe for many years we have neglected them because of the stigma society has placed on mental illness. When you are transparent, you will find your soul being drawn to those whose life is bound up tight and placed in our prison systems due to substance abuse. Troubled teens in our cities are often left for law enforcement to deal with, and many times, officers have not had the adequate training needed to help these teens.

I want to encourage you to continue living in your vulnerability. Living a safe life that doesn't allow you to be yourself is not a life of strength. If you are not comfortable in your own skin and have not owned your own story, then you do not have a life of strength and power. It is when you become weak in transparency and vulnerability that you become strong. We have turned vulnerability into a weakness in our society when, in reality, it is a strength.

Vulnerability gives you the strength to interact with other people and to empathize with them in their journey of heartache and pain. Is there a risk to vulnerability? Absolutely! However, the rewards of vulnerability far outweigh the risk.

The rewards of vulnerability far outweigh the risk

Your Vulnerability Overrides Your Susceptibility

Let's take a moment and talk about the susceptibility of vulnerability. A simple definition of vulnerability is to be susceptible to physical and mental harm and hurt. You are likely going to experience isolation from some when you become transparent and vulnerable. People that you once thought were your close friends may abandon you. They may think of you being a weak person if you admit to a past sin that had previously been hidden from them. Being isolated from those who you considered your friends is not a pleasant experience. I guess if people who you thought were your friends walk away from you, because you are transparent, then they really were never your friends.

Vulnerability may be painful, however, in your new walk of transparency, you will readily be connected to new friends. When you share your life openly, it will seem to your ultra conservative friends that you have become very liberal. If you have friends who live a life that is fake—in other words, they say they are decent people but are hiding a life of darkness—they may despise your being authentic with your life. This may say to them that you have a strength that they do not have. Some people will not want to be around you, thinking that something they are hiding in their lives might be exposed. You will often be criticized by those who have not had the courage to become vulnerable in sharing their life story. In the book of Matthew, there is a story of a woman being criticized for being vulnerable in the presence of Jesus.

> *And when Jesus was in Bethany at the house of Simon the leper, a woman came to Him having an alabaster flask of very costly fragrant oil, and she poured it on His head as He sat at the table. But when His disciples saw it, they were indignant, saying, "Why this waste? For this fragrant oil might have been sold for much and given to the poor. But when Jesus was aware of it, He said to them, "Why do you trouble the woman? For she has done a good work for Me. For you have the poor with you always, but Me you do not have always.*
> (Matt. 26:6–11)

This woman had opened her heart to Jesus and became very vulnerable with her actions. Make no mistake about it, she was very transparent in the open. She had opened her heart to Jesus by pouring this valuable oil upon His head. The disciples were indignant concerning what she had done. They criticized her by saying, "Why did you waste this oil on Him?" "We could have sold it for a lot of money and given it to the poor." They put a guilt trip on her that she did not deserve. I am sure emotionally she may have thought, *what terrible thing I have done to deserve their anger.* Jesus said to leave her alone and quit criticizing her for she has done a good work. In this story the principle is revealed that in your weakness, you become strong. With the words that Jesus spoke to the disciples, He gave her strength by saying she had done a good work.

This woman could have walked away in shame and defeat because of the way the disciples treated her. Instead, Jesus stepped up to the plate and honored her and defended her and placed her in a stronger position than the disciples were.

In your vulnerability, you will become susceptible to criticism. Brace yourself when you reach this stage of vulnerability for receiving treatment you never thought possible. People will say hurtful things to you and about you. They will do hurtful things to you in their anger. They will treat you like you never existed. I personally experienced this when I became transparent. Pastors, who were my peers, said things about me that were not true. They would say I had become a liberal-minded pastor, and there were those who even ostracized me from their group. These were pastors who I thought were my friends. Guess what, I had the privilege and honor of meeting new pastors who were real and authentic.

So, get this picture in your mind. You might think if this is happening to you that you are yielding to weakness. It would be natural for you to think this way. However, the Bible says in your weakness, you become strong. In your susceptibility, you become strong. In your vulnerability, you become strong. In your transparency, you become strong. Do you see the picture? I encourage you to get this picture in your mind. This is a biblical principle and will be fulfilled in your life. Your vulnerability will be stronger than your susceptibility.

Your Vulnerability Opens Your Heart

It is at this point when you open your heart to others and in your weakness that others will see God's strength in you. God has a lot to say about the human heart in the Word of God. It is important to understand the various principles concerning the heart. The book of Proverbs makes it clear that we are to guard our hearts because out of our hearts, life comes

When you guard your heart, you guard your life

forth. When you guard your heart, you guard your life. Your whole life story that you are owning today came forth and issued out of your heart. *"Keep your heart with all diligence, for out of it spring the issues of life"* (Prov. 4:23). A closed heart can never give or receive love and affection to any degree. Due to the fear of exposure, a closed heart wants to hide. It fears transparency and vulnerability. Consequently, it is a heart that retreats inwardly and puts up a guard around it, posting signs, reading "Do not enter."

We can appreciate the apostle Paul's challenge and encouragement concerning an open heart. Notice his challenge, encouragement, and admonition to the believers in the church at Corinth. *"Oh, dear Corinthian friends! We have spoken honestly with you, and our hearts are open to you. There is no lack of love on our part, but you have withheld your love from us. I am asking you to respond as if you were my own children. Open your hearts to us! (2 Cor. 6:11–13,* NLT). Paul covers a lot of territory in his statement to this church.

Paul makes it clear that he had opened his heart and became vulnerable to them. Paul's open heart exposed his life to these believers. It exposed the good, the bad, and the ugly segments of his life. He simply says, "I have been honest with you, and I have held nothing back". "This is my story, and I am going to own my story." His life story is interesting and very exciting. Paul was very open about his life before he came to know Christ as Savior and after he had His salvation experience on the road to Damascus.

Because of Paul owning his story and being very transparent, he becomes an encouragement to all of us about our vulnerability. Notice the statement I made about a closed heart not being able to receive or give love is confirmed in these verses. Paul points this out by saying, "I have shared love with you believers in Corinth, but you have withheld your love from me." Then Paul gives the reason why they were not expressing love to him. It is evident that their hearts were closed to him. He speaks to them like a father speaking to his children and admonishes them to open their hearts to him.

Notice in verse 11, the apostle Paul makes it clear that an open and transparent heart is one that is authentic—honest and not fake. Our culture is crying out for people like you with transparent hearts of honesty. Accepting lies as a way of life is being accepted in our culture today. A nation that accepts lying as a way of life will soon be living in bondage. It is somewhat rare to find people of honesty and authenticity in our culture today. Even in our churches today, we tend to ignore one of the Ten Commandments, "Thou shalt not lie." Paul continues in verse 12 by saying, "I have not held back my love from you in any way." However, in the same verse Paul states that they were not reciprocating his love. Let me ask you a question, why were they not extending their love to him? I believe the question is answered in verse 13. They had not opened their hearts to him. As a father to a child, he is challenging them to open their hearts to him.

Let me encourage you to embrace an open heart. If you are at the point of transformation and transparency, don't be afraid to open your heart and become vulnerable. Possibly you are at this point and in the process of opening your heart, and if so, let me encourage you to embrace and leverage your open-heart experience.

Jesus's Vulnerability Provides Your Strength

The life of Jesus is the greatest example we can follow to learn about life and how to write our life stories. In His transparency, He shows us through His own life what strength and power there is in vulnerability. The greatest weakness that you could ever experience is that of death. In death, every ounce of strength you have simply disappears. Jesus experienced the ultimate extent of losing His human strength when He died. Keep in mind He never lost His divine strength at death. He was still the omnipotent God but in His human form He died and lost His strength. The following verses record His vulnerability.

> *Let this mind be in you which was also in Christ Jesus, who, being in the form of God, did not consider it [robbery to be equal with God, but made Himself of no reputation, taking the form of a bondservant, and coming in the likeness of men. And being found in appearance as a man, He humbled Himself and became obedient to the point of death, even the death of the cross. Therefore, God also has highly exalted Him and given Him the name which is above every name, that at the name of Jesus every knee should bow, of those in heaven, and of those on earth, and of those under the earth, and that every tongue should confess that Jesus Christ is Lord, to the glory of God the Father.* (Phil. 2:5–11)

You find both His humility and vulnerability in the quoted scriptures. He humbled Himself by becoming an obedient man, and His vulnerability is seen in His death. Of course, His weakness of death was overridden by the strength of His resurrection. Not only is His strength seen in His resurrection, but God lifted Him and elevated Him to a position of honor. His name is lifted high, and every tongue will confess that He is Lord of all.

An open heart is a heart of love. You see t his love in the life and ministry of Jesus. Yes, it caused Him to experience vulnerability but in the same light, you can see it brought Him great satisfaction. In the life of Jesus,

An open heart is a heart of love

you see the three flexible characteristics of transparency. They are the two, humility and vulnerability, that we have now covered., and the third, *approachability*, that we will talk about in Chapter 9.

The love of God within your life will open many doors for you to be transparent and experience vulnerability. Agape love is a love that reaches out to those who often seem unreachable. Will you at times be hurt? I am sure that is a possibility and even a probability. Remember, even though you may not know how to reach out or what to say as you are reaching out in your vulnerability, that God's strength is always available to you. As you continue to write your story, make transparency a part of your daily page you are writing. You will find great satisfaction as you journey in a new-found strength.

As we leave the characteristic of vulnerability in this chapter, we will begin to find the golden nugget of life in our next chapter. What is that golden nugget? It is when you are so vulnerable that you become approachable to help other people write their story, using your story. Don't forget, own your story before your story owns you. In transparency, you have nothing to hide, no reason to look behind being worried about what someone might discover about your life. You are free and will experience the peace of being unshackled from the bondage of the past.

Probing and Pondering, Chapter Eight

WRITING YOUR STORY

- Your story line in Chapter 8: "Vulnerability"

"Instead, you ought to say, 'If the Lord wills,
we shall live and do this or that.'"
—James 4:15

EXPLORE: Study the scriptures to enhance your story line.

- *"Oh, dear Corinthian friends! We have spoken honestly with you, and our hearts are open to you. There is no lack of love on our part, but you have withheld your love from us. I am asking you to respond as if you were my own children. Open your hearts to us!"* (2 Cor. 6:11–13, NLT)

- *"And when Jesus was in Bethany at the house of Simon the leper, a woman came to Him having an alabaster flask of very costly fragrant oil, and she poured it on His head as He sat at the table. But when His disciples saw it, they were indignant, saying, "Why this waste? For this fragrant oil might have been sold for much and given to the poor. But when Jesus was aware of it, He said to them, "Why do you trouble the woman? For she has done a good work for Me. For you have the poor with you always, but Me you do not have always."* — *Matthew 26:6–11*

- *"Bear one another's burdens, and so fulfill the law of Christ."* —Galatians 6:2

ENGAGE: developing your story line

- *"Exposing your imperfections will make you vulnerable which in turn will make you accessible"* —Albert Schuessler

  1. Discuss the childhood vulnerability that Jesus experienced with His family and religious authorities.

  2. Discuss whether you agree with Paul that in weakness, you can become strong.

  3. Study and discuss how the Holy Spirit strengthens your inner person according to Ephesians 3:16

  4. Can you relate to a time when you experienced vulnerability because of your transparency?

  5. Have you shared an experience lately that you had hidden for years?

  6. Discuss the issue of mental illness in your group.

ENACT: applying to your story line

- *"Exchanging your weakness for God's strength is experienced in your vulnerability."* —Albert Schuessler

  1. Do you believe your prayer life would be beneficial when applying transparency?

  2. Allow the Holy Spirit to strengthen you inwardly.

  3. Exercise faith in God that He will strengthen you in your vulnerability.

EMPLOY: living out your story line

- *"Allow your transparency to take you places you never dreamed of going."*

    1. Challenge others to be transparent through your vulnerability.

    2. Open your heart of love to someone who is experiencing a lot of pain in their life.

    3. Think about being vulnerable to someone that is experiencing some form of mental illness.

Praying for ownership: Father, vulnerability can be uncomfortable at times. Sharing my weaknesses and failures is not easy, and I need Your power to do so. I pray You will empower me to think of what others are experiencing rather than be focused on my own interests. Father, encourage me to build a friendship with someone with mental health issues. Lord, challenge me to open my heart to minister to someone that is experiencing physical and emotional pain in their lives, and, Lord, strengthen me inwardly by the Holy Spirit.

CHAPTER 9

Approachability

"Blessed be the God and Father of our Lord Jesus Christ, the Father of mercies and God of all comfort, who comforts us in all our tribulation, that we may be able to comfort those who are in any trouble, with the comfort with which we ourselves are comforted by God"
—2 Corinthians 1:3–4

"Brethren, if a man is overtaken in any trespass, you who are spiritual restore such a one in a spirit of gentleness, considering yourself lest you also be tempted. Bear one another's burdens, and so fulfill the law of Christ. for if anyone thinks himself to be something, when he is nothing, he deceives himself."
—Galatians 6:1–3

"Approachability allows you to be a conduit
in helping others in writing their story."
—Albert Schuessler

"An open heart of transparency is the magnet that draws people to
your approachability."
—Albert Schuessler

"If hurting people hurt people then mended people mend people."
—Albert Schuessler

There are several words that can describe how transparency can affect our lives in a positive way. I am focusing on three words in the third part of this book. Humility and vulnerability are two words we have already discussed in chapters seven and eight. In this chapter, I want to highlight the word *approachability*. I believe being approachable to other people is one of the greatest rewards we will receive while passing through transformation on the way to becoming transparent. As a matter of fact, in the scriptures we see that our painful experiences are to be used in ministering to people who may be experiencing what we have experienced in the past. Oftentimes, God will use your experiences that He has worked out for good in your life to minister to other people to work out for good in their lives.

Come On In

Approachability comes from the Latin word *affabilis* that means coming near or approaching, kind, friendly, easily accessed, and open to conversation. The Greek word for approachable is *eggizo*, meaning to draw near or approach. A simple definition of approachability is a person who is approachable, friendly, easy to talk to, and has a quality of being reached. You have been around individuals who let you know right up front they are not approachable. You will recognize it in a look they may give you, or in some kind of gesture toward you. However, you may have approached someone with an issue you needed help with and discovered that this individual is beckoning you to *come on in*. They were friendly, open, approachable, and more than willing to enter your issue with you. You found you were comfortable with them.

Experiencing transparency opens a person up to becoming approachable to others who are hurting in their life journey. These hurting individuals often will approach you with a desire to enter your life for help. Since you have reached this level of approach-ability in your journey, you are now ready to step out and be that person that will say "*Come on in*" and let me help you with your hurt and your journey." You are inviting them to come into your life of openness. You now are an open invitation to those who are in need. "An open heart of transparency is the magnet that draws people to your approachability" (Albert Schuessler). This quote is on target concerning the magnetism you will have with the approachability you have earned through your transformation. This form of mag-netism is produced through the humility of your brokenness not through the pride of your self-centeredness. In the scriptures we see that God is a great example of this principle when He declares several times to humanity, *"Come on in."*

God's Says Come On In

There are several times in the Bible where God gives us an invi-tation to *"come on in."* In the book of Isaiah, He invites us to *come on in* and reason together with Him. *"Come now, and let us reason together,' Says the Lord, 'Though your sins are like scarlet They shall be as white as snow; Though they are red like crimson, they shall be as wool'"* (Isa. 1:18). People might visualize God as being stern, harsh, and unapproachable. Just the opposite is true. He has an open heart of love for anyone to come to Him. He has been more open to me than a lot of people and pastors have been to me in the past. Here is a righteous and holy God saying to sinners, *"Come on in* and let us talk about whatever is troubling you." I have come to visualize God in a way that I had never dreamed of or had ever been taught in the past. The brokenness journey has opened my eyes to a God who is approachable and is pleased when we come to Him for help. God only knows that we need Him all the time in our spiritual journey.

Notice the invitation God extends to us to find rest for our soul. *"Come to Me, all you who labor and are heavy laden, and I will give you rest. Take My yoke upon you and learn from Me, for I am gentle and lowly in heart, and you will find rest for your souls"* (Matt. 11:28–29). Since God created us, He knows what will trouble us and cause us to be loaded down with burdens. He invites us to *come on in,* and He will lighten our load and give us rest. This is called approachability. God is always open and approachable to you and to me. He is saying come toward Me, and you will find rest for your soul. When you read these verses, I want you to picture someone in the midst of their life cocoon with a heavy load and heavy heart, approaching God. It appears God is saying, "Let me in your cocoon with you, and I will provide rest for the struggle of your soul." I cannot imagine that God would ignore or would refuse to get inside your messy cocoon and help you sort it out. God can take your mess and sort it out for good for you to become the beautiful butterfly through your transformation.

"Let us therefore come boldly to the throne of grace, that we may obtain mercy and find grace to help in time of need" (Heb. 4:16). The writer of the book of Hebrews expresses even more dramatically God's invitation to *come on in.* When we are in the middle of a painful mess in our lives, we are apt to be ashamed and withdraw from others around us. We probably would be like Adam and Eve who were ashamed before God after they had sinned in the Garden of Eden. I remember in my time of depression, I was ashamed, scared, withdrawn from family and friends, alone, and lonely. We do not want anyone to see us in our painful circumstance. We never want anyone to see us in a weakened position in life. I felt somewhat

like Elijah when he was depressed, and God found him in the cave. He was hiding out in a dark cave, not wanting anyone to see him. God called him out and said to him, "Elijah, what are you doing in that cave?" God was saying to Elijah, "Approach me with whatever issue you may be dealing with in your life journey. You don't have to hide behind closed doors in shame anymore. You don't have to go it alone in your pain, so come boldly to me to find the help that you need." These words are spoken by one who is approachable to humanity.

Your Transparency Says Come On In

Being a child of God creates new characteristics within you that you have never experienced before. You become more like God in all that you say and do. If it is a characteristic of God to be accessible and approachable, then it is inherent for you to be accessible and approachable, as well. What that means for you as an individual is that you will be approachable to those in need, you must open your heart to hurting people, and you will become vulnerable in the world you are about to embark upon. It also means, in a positive way, that you will be like a beautiful butterfly, attracting those who are outcast, forlorn, ashamed, and rejected. Approachability is demanding on one hand and rewarding on the other hand. Approachability is both demanding and rewarding. It is demanding because you are about to enter someone's messy cocoon. When you enter someone's messy cocoon, you might get really dirty

Approachability is both demanding and rewarding

and become very vulnerable. It is rewarding because you will have the feeling of satisfaction that you are being an influence in someone else's story. Your approachability will be someone else's change-ability. That, my friend, is satisfying.

What does this approachability look like in the real world? How does that play out for you from a scriptural point of view? Keep in mind that God has a plan for you and your story. Your story is a process that unfolds with each significant event in your life. Whatever the event is, God uses it to bring you to the point of transparency for you to help others during their momentous events.

Your approachability will be someone else's changeability

I have found some of the most satisfying moments in my life is when I was able to share my story with someone who was crying out for help because they had absolutely no understanding of what was taking place in their life. They just knew they were hurting in their cocoon and didn't have an inkling of how to escape. I want to encourage you regarding your approachability with a few illustrations from the Bible that will challenge you to be approachable.

In the book of Galatians, the apostle Paul opens a door of opportunity for us to be approachable. Often our painful experiences in life are initiated by sin. *"Brethren, if a man is overtaken in any trespass, you who are spiritual restore such a one in a spirit of gentleness, considering yourself lest you also be tempted. Bear one another's burdens, and so fulfill the law of Christ. For if anyone thinks himself to be something, when he is nothing, he deceives himself"* (Gal. 6:1–3). In this scripture, Paul describes such a person as being overtaken by sin. How then do you come into the picture and help them with your transparency? One way is that you make yourself available to them and do all that you can to restore them back to where they need to be.

Notice Paul qualifies his statement by saying, "You who are spiritual, restore such a one." You might be saying, "I don't know if I would be considered spiritual or not." The point is this, spiritual growth happens through the process of brokenness and transformation. Your transparency is an indicator that you have grown spiritually and, in most cases, ready to enter that person's cocoon. If you notice in the balance of this scripture, Paul mentions that the one doing the restoring is to be gentle and humble, which are characteristics of a transformed believer. The picture Paul paints for us in this case is that someone needs to come alongside and help mend this individual who has succumbed to sin to their original state.

If hurting people hurt people, then mended people mend people. I believe that both scenarios are possible. In my counseling experience, I have found that oftentimes hurting people do hurt people. It could be hurting a spouse in a marriage. It might be a parent hurting a child. It is possible an employee is hurt by an employer. Here, again, is where you come into the picture with your approachability. You have escaped the cocoon and have been mended and now fly like a butterfly.

Your coming into the picture of helping someone that is hurting is much like God coming into the picture with Elijah. I think we underestimate how involved and detailed God is in our journey of life. My mind always goes back to the story of Elijah sitting under the broom tree, thinking life was coming to an end. I enjoy reading about the comfort Elijah received from God as the angels of the Lord provided him with cakes and a jar of water. I have mentioned this story in detail throughout this book for a reason. Elijah's story reveals quite clearly how God deals with us when we are down and out.

If you happen to be a person reading this book and are now transparent, I would encourage you to study Elijah's life story. I have shared my broom tree experience throughout this book. I remember how all I wanted was some release from my depression, knowing I needed comfort from somewhere or someone but had no idea where it was going to originate. I would buy books, thinking I might find the answer upon its pages, and I would read my Bible more, thinking that surely I would find the answer in this great book. I found myself praying unceasingly for the answer. I would seek counsel from my pastor friends, looking for them to provide an answer for me. Hours, days, weeks, months, and yes, a year went by before I realized my true comfort would come from God working in my life. I certainly received some answers from the wisdom found in the pages of the books I read. I received a tremendous amount of encouragement from my pastor friends that I relied upon. Praying and reading my Bible would provide me with principles and examples that were like the journey that I was on. However, the bottom line was the fact that God was the one that provided the comfort I needed.

I learned from the comfort I received in my cocoon. God climbed in the messy cocoon with me and provided true comfort for my soul. I learned transparency, and I learned approachability. The following verses taught me that the comfort I received in the cocoon is to be passed on to others who are looking for comfort. For that to happen means I must be approachable. God is going to use your mending to accomplish the mending in the lives of so many other people. *"Blessed be the God and Father of our Lord Jesus Christ, the Father of mercies and God of all comfort, who comforts us in all our tribulation, that we may be able to comfort those who are in any trouble, with the comfort with which we ourselves are comforted by God"* (2 Cor. 1:3–4). Now you are free, flying like a beautiful butterfly and enjoying the peace of God upon your life.

You name the pain, and you claim the gain

Let's look at what God has provided for you and what He wants you to do with this comfort experience. *First,* He has provided comfort for you. Notice the secret of the comfort you received is exposed, and now you know the secret is God Himself. It says that God is the God of all comfort. All means that no matter what your situation is and no matter what pain it may be creating, God can and will provide comfort for you. You name the pain, and you claim the gain. What comfort has God provided for you? *Secondly,* God challenges you to extend the comfort you received to someone you know who is in trouble. To have a clear understanding of the healing and comfort God has provided for you we must understand what the term means. The definition of comfort is the easing of a person's feelings, grief, or distress. It is defined as the ease and freedom from pain.

Notice the sequence of how your approachability will be beneficial in the life of someone going through troubling times in their life. Follow the pattern set forth in this scripture. You have gone through your brokenness and have been transformed through your messy cocoon. God entered your painful cocoon and comforted you in your trouble. The next step in the sequence says that you are now able to comfort others because of your experience coming out of the cocoon. The process is not as difficult as you might think. You might be thinking how can I be approachable and help someone else and that you are not an educated and trained counselor, coach, therapist, or pastor. What makes you approachable and influential is that you are educated and trained in your life story. You know firsthand what took place in your story—you know your story frontwards and backwards, which make you qualified to enter someone else's life story. Of course, there may be some situations where you will need to send them to a professional counselor for them to receive help in mental and physical issues.

Here is a list of things that might hold us back from being approachable. If an introvert saw someone approaching them with a life problem, they probably would step back into the shadows due to their shyness. A person filled with pride would consider it below their dignity for them to enter someone's messy cocoon. If an individual, who thinks they are super spiritual, would allow a sinner to approach them, they would probably succumb to peer pressure from their super-spiritual peers. A person of low self-esteem would not think they were worthy of helping someone else. Fear would overcome you if you lacked confidence in your giftedness. No one with a sinful hurt is going to approach a judgmental person because that person is not a safe place to share the secrets of their life. If you are a person who guards every second of your time in a day, you probably would not give a hurting person the time of day. If you came out of your cocoon a bitter person rather than a better person, you would have no clue on how to help someone else. Why? Because you have not owned your story at the present. You are still pouring salt in your wounds and do not have the salve to pour into the wounds of a hurting person.

Each person will react to their butterfly experience in their own way. No two people, no two painful situations, or no two cocoon experiences will be the same. Not only are they not the same, but no two personalities or temperaments are the same. Keep in mind your personality and temperament are not eliminated in the process; however, they may be tempered or modified during your transformation. In order not to fall prey to any of the things I have mentioned that might keep you from being accessible, you will need to take time to pray and think about your new butterfly role in life. Remember, you may not see yourself as adequate to be approachable to others, but God will empower and enable you to fulfill His call He has placed upon you. So, my advice is to step forward with open arms and trust God to enable you to enter the life story of one who is hurting in trials.

Jesus Practiced Come On In

There will always be someone who will try to talk you out of being approachable. It might be a family member, a friend, a spiritual leader, or even you yourself. Yes, you might be the one who would try to talk yourself out of being approachable. You will see in the following scriptures the disciples trying to talk Jesus out of being approachable to little children. "*Then little children were brought to Him that He might put His hands on them and pray, but the disciples rebuked them. But Jesus said, "Let the little children come to Me, and do not forbid them; for of such is the kingdom of heaven." And He laid His hands on them and departed from there*" (Matt. 19:13–15). The disciples rebuked the parents who brought the children to be blessed by Jesus. I can hear these disciples saying, "No, you can't bother Jesus; He is too busy. He is too important, and after all, He is God and can't be bothered by little kids." Obviously the disciples did not comprehend the approachability of Jesus Christ toward humanity. Notice in verse 14, Jesus said to the disciples let the children *come on in*. With Jesus, it was never about being more important than someone else. We certainly can learn from His example. Jesus was a humble man and did not think it was something to grasp to be important. You will see His humility in the following scriptures:

> *Let this mind be in you which was also in Christ Jesus, who, being in the form of God, did not consider it robbery to be equal with God, but made Himself of no reputation, taking the form of a bondservant, and coming in the likeness of men. And being found in appearance as a man, He humbled Himself and*

became obedient to the point of death, even the death of the cross." (Phil. 2:5–8)

In His humility, He became approachable to sinners and saints, unbelievers, and believers, rich and poor, the powerful and the weak. I encourage you to imitate Christ in His approachability with your approachability. The apostle Paul challenged us to imitate Christ as he imitated Christ *"Imitate me, just as I also imitate Christ"* (1 Cor. 11:1).

I've Opened the Door; Come On In

The flexibility of transparency has been the subject of Part 3 of this book. I have coupled together major characteristics of transparency in Part 3. They include three characteristics that transformation will produce in your butterfly experience. These three characteristics provide flexibility in your new, fulfilled life. These three characteristics are humility, vulnerability, and approachability. You may not realize it yet that these three characteristics provide you with the essence of enablement, where you find satisfaction in life. Think of this, you have made your life journey and have come to the place where you now own your story. You are free and living around so many people who are still chained and bound inside their messy cocoons.

My challenge to the reader of this book is to leverage your situation and pain for your benefit and for the benefit of others. Leverage means simply take advantage of owning your story. I am excited as I move into Part 4 and unfold for you the tremendous freedom you are or will be experiencing in the future. Everyone reading this book is to be found somewhere in the journey of this book. You may be going through the pain of *brokenness.* I will be praying for you. At this point in your journey, you may be experiencing the beauty of *transformation.* I will encourage you in the cocoon. You may be further down the road in your journey, and you have come to the point of the flexibility of *transparency*. I will fly with you. Keep putting one foot forward at a time and begin owning your story while you continue to write your story.

My final message to you in Part 3 is this. Don't stop now, the best is yet to come. When we finish Part 4, you will say, "Praise the Lord! Hallelujah, it has been worth the journey." God has a purpose and a plan for

Don't stop now, the best is yet to come

you, and the sooner you find out what it is, the sooner you will own your story for the glory of God. The final challenge: *come on in.*

Probing and Pondering, Chapter Nine

WRITING YOUR STORY

- Your story line in Chapter 9: "Approachability"

"Instead, you ought to say, 'If the Lord wills,
we shall live and do this or that.'"
—James 4:15

EXPLORE: Study the scriptures to enhance your story line.

- *"Blessed be the God and Father of our Lord Jesus Christ, the Father of mercies and God of all comfort, who comforts us in all our tribulation, that we may be able to comfort those who are in any trouble, with the comfort with which we ourselves are comforted by God"* —2 Corinthians 1:3–4

- *"Brethren, if a man is overtaken in any trespass, you who are spiritual restore such a one in a spirit of gentleness, considering yourself lest you also be tempted. Bear one another's burdens, and so fulfill the law of Christ. For if anyone thinks himself to be something, when he is nothing, he deceives himself."* — Galatians 6:1–3

ENGAGE: developing your story line

"Approachability allows you to be a conduit in helping
others in writing their story."
—Albert Schuessler

1. Discuss any experiences you have had when a hurting person approached you for counsel.

2. Discuss your thoughts about God possessing a *come on in* attitude.

3. Can you think of anything about your life that would hold you back from being open to approachability?

4. Discuss the following statement: If hurting people hurt people, then mended people mend people.

5. Exchange views about the sequence of comfort found in 2 Corinthians 1:3–4

6. Has there been a time in your life when you were ashamed to share the hurt and the pain you were experiencing?

ENACT: applying to your story line

"An open heart of transparency is the magnet that draws
people to your approachability."
—Albert Schuessler

1. Trust God that He will empower and enable you to become approachable.

2. Enhance these three characteristics in your life: Humility, vulnerability, and approachability.

3. Claim this principle that it was God who comforted you inside your messy cocoon.

EMPLOY: living out your story line

- "If hurting people hurt people, then mended people mend people." —Albert Schuessler

  1. Open your heart so wide that it would be easy for you to say *come on in.*

  2. Leverage your pain to become a mender of pain to others.

  3. Be determined to be that beautiful butterfly who attracts those who are still in their cocoon.

Praying for ownership: Father, give me the courage to be approachable. Open my heart to listen to Your heart when You are directing someone to approach me for counsel. I pray and ask You to empower me to be the butterfly of approachability that I need to be for You and for others. Father, I thank You for the comfort You provided during my time in the cocoon. I praise You for the transparency I am experiencing at the present time.

PART 4

The Living Life Abundantly

P art 4 of this book is what I call the cream that rises to the top of brokenness. Let me explain from scripture why I call it the cream that rises to the top. *"The thief does not come except to steal, and to kill, and to destroy. I have come that they may have life, and that they may have it more abundantly"* (John 10:10). This scripture describes the up-and-down experiences you will have in life. It includes the negative and the positive realities of living. The thief refers to the Devil who comes to steal, kill, and destroy. He will use the pain of your brokenness to steal your joy and peace and will make every attempt possible to kill your spirit and destroy your dreams. You have seen that scenario played out in this book many times up to this point. What I have described is the negative side of life. However, in this scripture you will see a positive side to life, as well. Jesus makes it clear He has come to give you life.

I came to know Christ when I was eight years old. The Bible says that whosoever calls upon the Lord shall be saved. When I called upon the Lord, I was given life. However, I found even though I had life, something was still missing deep inside me. The peace and joy of the Lord was often absent from my everyday experiences. While

I was amid brokenness and passing through the messy cocoon of transformation, my spiritual eyes were opened to what I was missing. When I broke loose from the cocoon and was free to fly like a butterfly, the transparency I experienced at that moment allowed me to see more clearly what I was missing. It was at this point I realized that my life journey had always stopped at the comma after the word *life* in this verse. As you can see, on the other side of the comma is the abundant life. Jesus came to give us abundant life. The abundant life is the cream that rises to the top. The final three chapters of this book will be describing what the cream that rises to the top of brokenness really looks like in your journey.

CHAPTER 10

A Joyful Heart

"You will show me the path of life; In Your presence is fullness of joy;
At Your right hand are pleasures forevermore."
—Psalm 16:11

"These things I have spoken to you, that My joy may remain in you,
and that your joy may be full."
—John 15:11

"May the God of hope fill you with all joy and peace in believing,
that you may abound in hope by the power of the Holy Spirit."
—Romans 15:13

"Enjoy the transcending joy of Christ's joy."
—Albert Schuessler

"When you choose joy as your medicine,
most hurts will be healed in your heart."
—Albert Schuessler

"Joy can provide light to lift your soul above the
clouds of darkness hanging over you."
—Albert Schuessler

W hen you own your story, you will begin to see the cream of brokenness rising to the top of your journey. You will see and understand the life that God has intended for you to live and the life you have so much longed for in your journey. It is what John calls the abundant life. *"The thief does not come except to steal, and to kill, and to destroy. I have come that they may have life, and that they may have it more abundantly"* (John 10:10). Your brokenness, transformation, and transparency will carry you across the threshold to enter into an abundant life. It is what I call getting past the comma in John 10:10 and moving from life to the abundant life. Some of the cream that rises to the top of brokenness is experiencing a joyful heart. Let me explain what I mean by cream rising to the top.

I can remember years ago when the dairyman would take a pail of fresh milk from the cow and pour it into a hand-operated milk separator and separate the cream from the milk. The cream in the pail would always rise to the top of the pail. The cream was delicious. The cream on top was the best tasting thing in that pail. I can still remember pouring cream on a bowl of cereal or a bowl of strawberries. I can recall my mother using an eggbeater and whipping that cream into whipped cream. It was so much richer and tastier than the packaged whipped cream you buy in the store today. I would rather have cream on my cereal than milk. Why? To me it was the best of the two. The phrase *"the cream rising to the top"* has come to represent that the best will rise to the top. In our case, brokenness will provide you with the abundant life, which is the best, and it will rise to the top in your story. One aspect of the best of the abundant life is to acquire a joyful heart.

Brokenness and transformation will always draw you to God and to His plan and purpose for your life. Your brokenness is what will carry you across the comma from life to the abundant life as described in John 10:10. The abundant life is defined by the things we so much want in life but cannot seem to attain. These are things you cannot earn or buy. We often try to obtain them through means that cannot produce them. We think we can experience them through riches, possessions, prestige, entertainment, or family.

What are these things that seem to escape us most of the time? They are joy of the heart, peace of the mind, and rest for the soul. These three things can be provided for us only by the grace of God. In this chapter, we are going to focus on a joyful heart. Where is this joy to be found and how can I apply joy to my life? You won't find it; you will be drawn to it through your brokenness and transformation. God will apply it to your life as you are drawn to Him.

Joy in His Presence

Joy will be experienced while in the presence of God. *"You will show me the path of life; In Your presence is fullness of joy; At Your right hand are pleasures forevermore"* (Ps. 16:11). In the Old Testament, the Hebrew word for joy is *simchah,* which means glee, gladness, pleasure, and rejoicing. In the New Testament, the Greek word for joy is *chara,* which means calm, delight, cheerfulness, and gladness. You will find that Psalm 16:11 is filled with gems to be desired by just about anyone. Notice the promises of God woven throughout this verse. *First,* He promises to show us the path of life. This is speaking of the journey you are traveling today. No matter what leg of the journey you are on at the present time, He promises to direct each step that you take. Keep in mind He has a path, a purpose, and a plan for you to travel. *Secondly,* this verse speaks of the fullness of joy to be found in His presence. In this profound statement, it says fullness of joy is in His presence. Fullness is a great definition of what abundantly means. The Greek word for fullness is *perissos* which means beyond measure, exceedingly, superior, and excessive. The abundant life is a life filled with God's joy. I suppose we might find happiness if we were to win the lottery, land a new job, purchase a new car, score a hole-in-one on the golf course, or receive an award for a great accomplishment. Remember this one thing, fullness of joy, is found only in the presence of God. Your brokenness and transformation draw you into the presence of God where you will discover this joy. *Thirdly,* the last statement in Psalm 16:11 states that at God's right hand there are pleasures forevermore. Ponder upon this statement for a moment. Let the depth of its meaning sink deep into your soul; there are pleasures forevermore at His right hand while amid His presence.

Can you imagine that the brokenness you have experienced and your survival out of the messy cocoon can provide you with an abundant life. It can and will provide you with the fullness of

Your brokenness will provide you with fullness of joy

joy. Your brokenness will provide you with fullness of joy. This joy can be a reality in your life if you choose to own your story and to leverage your story for the glory of God. However, if you choose to become bitter rather than better because of your brokenness, you will never encounter God's unspeakable joy. I pray you have chosen to be drawn to the presence of God, and His joy is full within your heart today.

Let me recap the great promises in Psalm 16:11 for you. God promises to show you the path of life. He is continually directing your path in accordance with His purpose and plan for your journey. Remember the title of chapter 1 is "I'm in control." The question I have for you is how did that go? There was no plan or purpose to life when we were in control. However, God's plan and purpose is found in chapter 3 titled "God's in Control." When God is in control, He will show you the way of life, which will bring about a heart filled with joy. The next promise is that there is joy in the presence of God. The last promise is that there is pleasure forevermore at His right hand.

Joy in Abiding in Jesus

It is a thrill to be writing this chapter because I know the joy that is available to you through your brokenness. This joy will advance you forward in your abundant life. In this abiding in Christ section, you will find a new jewel to add to your collection of God's gems. Notice God's new promises in the following verse: *"These things I have spoken to you, that My joy may remain in you, and that your joy may be full"* (John 15:11). Actually, there are two promises in this verse. He makes it clear that the joy we so much desire is *His* joy in us. This is an important point when it comes to true joy. True joy is not something we conjure up on our own through our own efforts. In the next statement, it is stated, that because of His joy, our joy will be full. Again, the word *full* is speaking of an abundant joy which, in turn, produces an abundant life.

The context of John 15:1–11 is our abiding in the Lord Jesus Christ. Abiding in Christ is like being in the presence of God. Being found abiding in Christ will pay great dividends. It is this dwelling in Christ where you will draw from His joy, and consequently, your joy will be full. It is important to remember that it is your brokeness that has brought you to this dwelling place

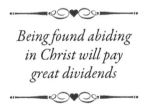

Being found abiding in Christ will pay great dividends

I am the true vine, and My Father is the vinedresser.
Every branch in Me that does not bear fruit He takes
away; and every branch that bears fruit He prunes,

that it may bear more fruit. You are already clean because of the word which I have spoken to you. Abide in Me, and I in you. As the branch cannot bear fruit of itself, unless it abides in the vine, neither can you, unless you abide in Me. "I am the vine; you are the branches. He who abides in Me, and I in him, bears much fruit; for without Me you can do nothing. If anyone does not abide in Me, he is cast out as a branch and is withered; and they gather them and throw them into the fire, and they are burned. If you abide in Me, and My words abide in you, you will ask what you desire, and it shall be done for you. By this My Father is glorified, that you bear much fruit; so, you will be My disciples. "As the Father loved Me, I also have loved you; abide in My love. If you keep My commandments, you will abide in My love, just as I have kept My Father's commandments and abide in His love. "These things I have spoken to you, that My joy may remain in you, and that your joy may be full."
(John 15:1–11)

What does abiding mean to you in real time? We are admonished to abide in Christ in the context of this scripture. What does abiding in Christ convey to you in your journey of brokenness and transformation? What does it mean while you are dying to self in the cocoon? What might abiding express to you while you are fluttering through space as a butterfly? What does abiding mean in your life of transparency? What does abiding in Christ signify to you at the present time as you are experiencing the abundant life? The Greek word for abide is *meno* which means to stay in a given place, to dwell, to remain, to be present, and to tarry. So, no matter what segment of your journey you find yourself in today, be encouraged to remain and dwell in the presence of Christ to find joy within that stage.

Notice in the following scripture Jesus states that everything He spoke of in John 15:1–10 had a life purpose behind it: *"These things I have spoken to you, that My joy may remain in you, and that your joy may be* full" (John 15:11). He speaks of His joy remaining in us. Contemplate upon what Jesus is saying to you in this scripture. He doesn't say joy like His or similar to His; no, it is His joy that will remain in you. It is interesting to note that Jesus was a man of sorrows and grief. He is described as a man beaten, rejected, despised, afflicted, and ultimately crucified. However, in Hebrews 12:2, it says *"Who for the joy that was set before Him endured the cross."* How do you reconcile these two very different statements made about Jesus in the Bible? It certainly teaches us that there can be joy in the face of rejection, affliction, pain, and sorrow. The Bible calls it joy unspeakable and full of glory. It is a joy that is an eternal joy because Jesus is an eternal being. It may seem like what you are facing today is going to last for eternity but remember that His joy is an everlasting joy.

Joy unspeakable and full of glory

I recall, as I was going through the cocoon stage of my journey, that there were many times I would cry out to God, seeking relief from my emotional pain. I would find myself in places where I was alone, and no one knew my location. I was deep in thought and in prayer, asking God for peace, tranquility, and joy. Everyone around me knew that I did not have joy in my life. My countenance revealed the sadness that was rooted deep within my heart. I did not realize at the time that God was reaching out to me by inviting me to seek and ask Him for His joy. *"And in that day you will ask Me nothing. Most assuredly, I say to you, whatever you ask the Father in My name*

He will give you. Until now you have asked nothing in My name. Ask, and you will receive, that your joy may be full" (John 16:23–24).

I guess sometimes we must be down and out before we pray and ask God to give us His joy. I can remember the day that I was able to break loose from my year-long depression. It was like being released from the shackles of bondage. The hurt and heaviness that I had experienced in my heart everyday was gone. That emotional pain in the center of my chest was as painful as any physical pain. Suddenly it was lifted, and the sadness it created was lifted as joy filled my heart for the first time in my life. I found myself passing over the comma in John 10:10 and encountering the abundant life. I would like to say that I live an abundant life daily, but there are times it slips away from me. However, my previous experiences of brokenness and transformation always guides me back to an abundant life.

Joy in the Power of the Holy Spirit

To highlight the fact that true joy comes from God, I want to bring the third person of the Trinity into the conversation. Joy is yours when you are in the presence of God, when you are abiding in Christ, and when you are living in the power of the Holy Spirit. In the following verse, the writer once again speaks of being filled with joy and peace. *"May the God of hope fill you with all joy and peace in believing, that you may abound in hope by the power of the Holy Spirit"* (Rom. 15:13). The writers seem to emphasize the words *fullness, full* and *filled* in the verses we have looked at to highlight the abundance of joy available to us.

It is important to include the work and power of the Holy Spirit in your abundant life journey. It is logical and reasonable to include the fullness of the Holy Spirit in your life if you are going to assimilate joy within your hearts. When you become a believer in Christ, the Bible says that immediately the Holy Spirit enters your spirit, and you are born again. Therefore, the Spirit of God dwells within your spirit and will always be there day and night to empower you in your life journey. It is the Holy Spirit that empowers your brokenness and transformation to break the chains of your cocoon and to release you as a butterfly to experience the joy of an abundant life. It is the Holy Spirit that draws you into the presence of God, and it is He that directs you in abiding in Christ. As the scripture declares, the hope of joy and peace is empowered by the Holy Spirit of God in your life.

Once you have been there and know firsthand what an abundant life feels like, you can now begin to understand how it came about in your life. There are certain spiritual laws or principles that we live by, according to the Word of God. For instance, in the following verse, there is a promise laid out for those who walk in the Spirit: *"There is therefore now no condemnation to those who are in Christ Jesus, who do not walk according to the flesh, but according to the Spirit"* (Rom. 8:1). The promise of no condemnation is based upon two divine laws. The word *law* can be synonymous to the word *principle*. In other words, there are two principles laid out for us in the following verse: *"For the law of the Spirit of life in Christ Jesus has made me free from the law of sin and death"* (Rom. 8:2).

In the natural world, one law can override another law. An example would be that the law of aerodynamics can override the law of gravity. An example in the spiritual world is that the *"law or principle of the spirit of life in Christ Jesus has made us free from the law* (or principle) *of sin and death."* As these principles take place in your journey, your brokenness begins to work for good in your life, and you find a new freedom through your transformation. The principle of the Spirit of life in Christ Jesus has overridden the principle of sin and death. This principle frees you from living in sin and all the pain it causes in your life. In doing so, it gives you a boost over the comma and draws you to God and into His presence where you find the fullness of joy.

You will find that one of the nine attributes of the Holy Spirit of God is joy. *"But the fruit of the Spirit is love, joy, peace, longsuffering, kindness, goodness, faithfulness, gentleness, self-control. Against such there is no law"* (Gal. 5:22–23). Joy is a part of the total makeup of the Holy Spirit. This joy that is His is dispersed throughout your being as you walk in the Spirit. Since He is God, you are therefore in the presence of God where joy is to be found. The Bible speaks of the Spirit of Christ abiding in you providing joy as well. *"But you are not in the flesh but in the Spirit, if indeed the Spirit of God dwells in you. Now if anyone does not have the Spirit of Christ, he is not His. And if Christ is in you, the body is dead because of sin, but the Spirit is life because of righteousness"* (Rom. 8:9–10). You can clearly see that divine joy transcends human joy and provides you with a joyful heart.

Divine joy transcends human joy

I want to provide you with a visual that will picture how God's joy transcends your joy. It is a picture of a vine and its branches, a picture of how the nutrients flow from the tap root through the trunk out into the branches and ultimately bearing fruit. The relationship between the Father, His Son, and His children is pictured as a vineyard. God the Father is the gardener, Jesus is the vine itself, and the believer is a branch: *"I am the true vine, and My Father is the vinedresser."* (John 15:1) In the following verse, it makes it clear we can do nothing without Jesus. *"I am the vine; you are the branches. He who abides in Me, and I in him, bears much fruit; for without Me you can do nothing."* (John 15:5) Here you see a picture painted in this chapter of joy that is found in the presence of God, abiding in Christ, and empowered by the Holy Spirit. The nutrients that feed your joy that you experience in your abundant life comes from the tap root, which is Christ Jesus. Christ life flows through the root into the branch, which is you, and produces the fruit of His joy in you so your joy may be full. "*If you keep My commandments, you will abide in My love, just as I have kept My Father's commandments and abide in His love. "These things I have spoken to you, that My joy may remain in you, and that your joy may be full.*" (John 15:10-11) This is the process of divine joy transcending human joy.

Experiencing the joy of Christ in your transparency is one step closer to jumping over the comma hurdle found after the word *life* in John 10:10 and experiencing the abundant life. "*The thief does not come except to steal, and to kill, and to destroy. I have come that they may have life, and that they may have it more abundantly*" (John 10:10). No doubt, human joy can be found in secular life as well as spiritual life, but abundant joy can only be found in our personal abiding relationship with the divine Trinity—God the Father, Son, and Holy Spirit. I believe so many people have life, but the abundant life seems to escape them like it did me for so many years. The joy seems to be missing in the life of so many believers in our culture today. Of course, we might have a smile on our face, a little laughter now and then, and a cheerful personality. The principles discovered here is that brokenness produces transformation, transformation brings about transparency, and the three together gives rise to the joy of an abundant life that produces a joyful heart. Enjoy the transcending joy of Christ's joy.

Probing and Pondering, Chapter Ten

WRITING YOUR STORY

- Your story line in Chapter 10: "A Joyful Heart"

"Instead, you ought to say,; If the Lord wills,
we shall live and do this or that."
—James 4:15

EXPLORE: Study the scriptures to enhance your story line.

- *"The thief does not come except to steal, and to kill, and to destroy. I have come that they may have life, and that they may have it more abundantly."* —John 10:10

- *"You will show me the path of life; In Your presence is fullness of joy; At Your right hand are pleasures forevermore"* — Psalm 16:11

- *"These things I have spoken to you, that My joy may remain in you, and that your joy may be full."* —John 15:11

- *"May the God of hope fill you with all joy and peace in believing, that you may abound in hope by the power of the Holy Spirit."* —Romans 15:13

ENGAGE: developing your story line

- "When you choose joy as your medicine, most hurts will be healed in your heart." —Albert Schuessler

  1. Did the comma in John 10:10 ever hold you back from advancing spiritually?

2. How would you describe to others what being in the presence of God means to you?

3. Discuss the difference between divine joy and human joy.

4. What might produce human joy, and what might produce divine joy in your life?

5. Discuss your thoughts about the vine and the branch relationship to abiding in the joy of Christ.

6. Share a time when you first experienced the fullness of joy in your life.

ENACT: applying to your story line

- "Enjoy the transcending joy of Christ's joy." —Albert Schuessler

  1. Consider ways you can become more knowledgeable about the fullness of Christ's joy.

  2. Are there areas in your life that you could be more yielded to the Holy Spirit to experience His joy?

  3. Learn to draw your spiritual nutrients from God's spiritual tap root in order to bear joyful fruit.

  4. Choose to make living an abundant life a top priority in your spiritual life.

EMPLOY: living out your story line

- "Joy can provide light to lift your soul above the clouds of darkness hanging over you." —Albert Schuessler

1. Help the sad around you to experience joy through their brokenness.

2. Help people to understand how their intellectual knowledge can provide the experiential knowledge needed to live an abundant life.

3. Spread your joy around in a culture filled with great sadness.

4. Fully live the abundant life to bring glory to God.

Praying for ownership: Father, I want to thank You for the joy I have had the privilege of experiencing in my life. In Your presence, I find a life filled with joy and satisfaction. I am grateful that Your spiritual nutrients flow through Jesus into my life through the Holy Spirit. I pray You will direct me to those who are going through brokenness and empower me to share Your love, joy, and peace with them. Thank You, Jesus, for Your abundant life being lived through me at the present time.

CHAPTER 11

A Restful Soul

*"God's promise of entering his rest still stands, so we ought to tremble
with fear that some of you might fail to experience it."*
—Hebrews 4:1 NLT

*"Come to Me, all you who labor and are heavy laden, and I will give
you rest. Take My yoke upon you and learn from Me, for I am gentle
and lowly in heart, and you will find rest for your souls.
For My yoke is easy and My burden is light."*
—Matthew 11:28–30

*"Those who live in the shelter of the Most High will find rest in the
shadow of the Almighty. This I declare about the Lord: He alone is
my refuge, my place of safety; he is my God, and I trust him."*
—Psalm 91:1–2, NLT

*"This is what the Lord says: "Stop at the crossroads and look around.
Ask for the old, godly way, and walk in it. Travel its path, and you
will find rest for your souls. But you reply, '
'No, that's not the road we want!"*
—Jeremiah 6:16, NLT

"When you seek rest for your restless soul would you consider
finding it inside a yoke?"
—Albert Schuessler

"Yielding to God's direction in your travel is
important in finding rest for your soul."
—Albert Schuessler

"Your transformation in the cocoon is your transportation
to the yoke of Jesus Christ."
—Albert Schuessler

A pastor friend of mine called me one day a few years ago to chat about what was happening in our ministries. Like any conversation, we were back and forth talking about both the bad and the good things that were happening in our churches at the time. The conversation went on for about fifteen minutes with small talk, laughing, and joking. I guess I must have come across with a negative attitude as the conversation progressed. If I remember correctly, I believe I had started to complain, gripe, and grumble about my ministry and my life in general. I will never forget what my pastor friend said to me in the middle of our conversation. He said, "Al, what is the matter with you? You seem to be agitated for some reason, and you come across as being very restless." The next statement is the one that got my attention when he said: "Hey man, aren't you in Jesus's yoke where you are supposed to be resting in Him?" Jokingly, I said, "Shut up, I don't have to listen to you!" I realized at that moment I had been caught in my restlessness because of my behavior. I knew he was exactly right in his analysis that I was not resting my soul in the yoke of Jesus.

I see a lot of restlessness in our culture today both in and out of the church walls. I meet people who are tired both physically and spiritually. The lack of a restful soul is apparent immediately when you run across a person who is dragging physically and spiritually. We will be highlighting in this chapter on how to have spiritual rest for your soul. I believe when we are at rest in our soul, that rest will transfer rest into our bodies. So much of our physical pain is caused by the psychological condition of our mind. Keep in mind that when I speak of the soul, I am speaking of the mind, emotions, and the will, or as some call it the inner person. Our inner person must be cared for in order for us to be strong. We must nurture our inner person. One of the blessings received from brokenness and transformation is the strengthening of your inner person as described in the following

We must nurture our inner person

verse: *"that He would grant you, according to the riches of His glory, to be strengthened with might through His Spirit in the inner man"* (Eph. 3:16). When your mind is cared for and you are strong inwardly, this will provide rest for you physically and spiritually.

The mind is at rest when it ceases to be disturbed and agitated. The mind is very powerful and complex. I believe it is in the soul, the inner person—the mind, emotions, and will—where you actually live. That is why the Bible gives us clear instruction on what our thinking pattern should be like. In defining biblical rest, it is important to understand that it is speaking more about experiencing spiritual rest than physical rest. One important fact about biblical rest is that it is not speaking about cessation from labor. Normally this is how most of us would define physical rest. Biblical rest is defined as an inward rest in your soul while you are laboring. It is finding restoration of lost strength, which is an inner rest experienced simultaneously in labor. It is a working rest, one that you cannot buy, but the Holy Spirit alone can provide for you. It is a rest that one experiences in the service of Christ when we stop thinking we are so important and great.

Rest for the Lost Soul

While you are reading this book, you may begin to realize that you are not a believer in Christ. I would like to share some life-changing thoughts with you about finding rest for your soul in Christ Jesus. You may be someone who is *not sure* if you are a believer in Christ, and I would like to share with you how you can know for sure you are resting in Him. There are many people who will say to me that they *think* they are believers in Christ. If you are in this category, I would like to help you settle this question in your mind so that you can know that you are a believer in Christ. In the following verse, God makes it clear that spiritual rest for your soul is readily available to you today: *"God's promise of entering his rest still stands, so we ought to tremble with fear that some of you might fail to experience it"* (Heb. 4:1, NLT). This moment may be the time in your life journey that you need to take that first step in finding rest for your soul. Today may be the day for those who doubt your salvation that you can settle in your mind that without a shadow of doubt you are a believer in Christ.

Here is God's plan for you to find rest for your soul by believing in the finished work of Jesus Christ upon the cross: *"that if you confess with your mouth the Lord Jesus and believe in your heart that God has raised Him from the dead, you will be saved. For with the heart one believes unto righteousness, and with the mouth confession is made unto salvation"* (Rom. 10:9–10). Not only does God give you eternal life and the rest for your soul that comes with it, but He wants you to know without a shadow of doubt that you have eternal life as noted in the following verses: *"And this is what God has testified: He has given us eternal life, and this life is in his Son. Whoever has the Son has life; whoever does not have God's Son does not have life. I have written this to you who believe in the name of the Son of God, so that you may know you have eternal life"* (1 John 5:11–13).

I encourage you to take a moment from reading this book and analyze where you are in your spiritual life. Ask yourself some questions about your relationship with God. Do you have peace with God and rest for your soul? These are hard questions to face and harder to answer. I believe the most important decision we will ever make in life is to receive Jesus Christ into our lives. When we accept Him as our Savior, it takes the agitation and despair out of our soul and replaces it with rest. Whatever you do, do not miss out on the rest for your soul that God has for you.

Brokenness Cures Restlessness

When you look back on your journey and brokenness was happening in your life, you probably shudder at the thought of you being at war with God and yourself. That war was brought about by the conflict you were experiencing over who is going to be in control of your life. I can remember well how restless my soul was when going through my brokenness. I was angry, agitated, hurting, anxious, edgy, troubled, and uptight. Rest for my soul was nowhere in sight nor to be found, so I thought. I found that I was wrong in my thinking at the time. It was at that very moment when God took control of my life that I experienced something new for the very first time. What did I experience? My soul was at rest, no more war tormenting me day and night. I did not find this rest on my own. I found it in the shadow of Almighty God. *"Those who live in the shelter of the Most High will find rest in the shadow of the Almighty.*

This I declare about the Lord: He alone is my refuge, my place of safety; he is my God, and I trust him" (Ps. 91:1–2, NLT).

You may recall in your situation where you found your life had transformed from living in the shadows of who you thought you were to living in the shadow of the Almighty God. Suddenly you found your soul was at rest. Immediately the agitation, edginess, pain, and anxiety were gone. It is a day in which you will never forget when you found rest for your soul. You stopped at the crossroads, looked around, and chose to travel in the direction God wanted you to travel. It is valuable to stop at the crossroads and look around. You accomplished this by turning loose of the wheel of your life and allowed God to be at the helm of your life journey. *"This is what the Lord says: 'Stop at the crossroads and look around. Ask for the old, godly way, and walk in it. Travel its path, and you will find rest for your souls.' But you reply, 'No, that's not the road we want!'"* (Jer. 6:16, NLT). The brokenness and transformation are what carried you across the comma in John 10:10 and favored you with the abundant life. In doing so, it produced in you a restful soul.

> *It is valuable to stop at the crossroads and look around*

Jesus's Yoke Provides Rest

It is difficult for me to imagine how anyone could find rest in a yoke, serving alongside Jesus. A yoke is defined as a wooden beam placed upon the neck of an oxen in order to pull a load. That sounds like labor to me. The following scripture paints an unusual picture about rest for your soul. *"Come to Me, all you who labor and are heavy laden, and I will give you rest. Take My yoke upon you and learn from Me, for I am gentle and lowly in heart, and you will find rest for your souls. For My yoke is easy and My burden is light"* (Matt. 11:28–30). Finding yourself in Christ's yoke is where brokenness has taken you. Your transformation in the cocoon is your transportation to be found in the yoke of Jesus Christ. Once you're in the yoke, the abundant life is now available for you to find rest for your soul. Thus, you find a restful soul to enjoy.

Notice the invitation given to those who are wrestling with issues and are loaded down with cares, anxiety, agitation, edginess, and fear in your soul. If you will accept Jesus's invitation and come to Him, He will fulfill this promise. As I read this scripture, I think of the times that I thought I could produce rest for my soul by my own efforts. After all, I am a smart guy, I can figure out life on my own, I can get the job done. I can tell you right now in my transparency that getting the job done on my own didn't quite work out as I had planned. Why do we labor on our own when we can tag along with Jesus in His yoke? He makes it clear that His yoke is easy, and His burden is light. He declares that He is gentle and lowly in heart. Everything that He says about Himself, and His yoke is totally opposite of an agitated, edgy, and anxious soul. Just about everything that would describe a restless soul is found in these verses. These are issues we struggle with daily and sometimes for years. Circumstances can become laborious and be a heavy load within our soul.

I believe Jesus has humanity figured out with what He says about our inner soul. We don't pull the wool over Jesus's eyes at all, He knows the struggles of people. In the following scripture, James outlines the struggle that Jesus is aware of taking place in our souls.

> *Where do wars and fights come from among you?*
> *Do they not come from your desires for pleasure that*
> *war in your members? You lust and do not have. You*

> *murder and covet and cannot obtain. You fight and*
> *war. Yet you do not have because you do not ask. You*
> *ask and do not receive, because you ask amiss, that*
> *you may spend it on your pleasures.* (James 4:1–3)

James now describes the inner struggle that we are faced with and experience daily, describing the struggle as a war where there is fighting taking place. We often think that the war is with other people or painful situations we may be experiencing. These are fights we experience on the surface, but the restlessness of the soul goes much deeper. James reveals that the struggles are due to our desires for pleasure that war within our members. He says we are just like the caterpillar, living a life feeding the appetite of the lust of the flesh. Like the caterpillar, we want to fulfill our appetite so we can continue to live in our pleasures that cause our restlessness. Our restlessness that James is describing is because we want to be in control. He says you don't have it because you ask amiss, or for the wrong reason. The reason you are asking for something is because you want it to fulfill your lustful pleasure. Remember chapter one of this book, "I'm in Control." Being in control of our lives will always produce a certain restlessness in our soul. The life James is describing here in the context of this scripture certainly does not describe the abundant life.

The yoke spoken of is a double yoke where two oxen would be yoked together with a collar around their neck. It now becomes more clearer as to the necessity of being found in Christ's yoke. Here are just a few important principles we learn from His yoke. *First,* it means that Christ is in control, we are along for the restful ride, and the struggles James speaks of will be eliminated from our journey. *Secondly,* though we are yoked together, He is the one who is pulling the load, and we are serving with Him and resting in our labor with

Him. *Thirdly,* He is the one deciding the direction you should be traveling in your journey, so you are traveling in the same direction He is going, and *fourthly,* He is gentle and His yoke is light in order for you to bear the load you are experiencing. He will not go faster than you can go. He will not put a heavier load upon the yoke than that which you can handle. He will not take you in a direction that is not suited for you.

His promise in these verses is that He is gentle, lowly in heart, His yoke is easy, His burden is light, and you will find rest for your soul because He will give you rest for your soul. The yoke then becomes an ideal setting for us to live the abundant Christian life. You and Christ yoked together can accomplish more in your life journey than if you decide to do life in your single yoke while pulling the entire load yourself. Jesus expresses in this scripture to take His yoke upon you. There is a choice to be made concerning the yoke of Jesus Christ that will leave room for you to decide not to take the yoke and do life totally under your control..

I pray that through your brokenness, you have been transformed and are now living the abundant Christian life. I pray that right now you have a restful soul because you have given up control of your life and are resting in the yoke of Christ. If you are not living the abundant life, then where does your life feel burdened today? What is the burden upon your soul that you are carrying alone? In what area does your life feel so heavy that you sense the struggle within your soul? Do you feel loneliness in your life by carrying your burden alone? You do not have to bear your burdens alone. If these question marks belong to you, then listen to what Peter says about these question marks. He says, *"casting all your care upon Him, for He cares for you"* (1 Pet. 5:7). Peter is simply saying, take

You do not have to bear your burdens alone

the wars and fighting that you are struggling with and cast them into the yoke of Christ. The choice we have is to take these question marks and try to answer them on our own, or cast them upon Jesus and let Him answer them according to His way which leads to an abundant life.

God's Control Imparts Rest

As I think about being in Christ's yoke, it brings my mind back to chapter 3 of this book titled "God's in Control." The following verses lay out with great clarity for us to understand what the yoke principle looks like in our life: *"Trust in the Lord with all your heart, and lean not on your own understanding; In all your ways acknowledge Him, and He shall direct your paths"* (Prov. 3:5–6). These verses are filled with so many gems describing the path to an abundant life:

- *Trust in the Lord with all your heart.* It takes a tremendous amount of trust to place your life in His yoke.

- *Lean not on your own understanding.* This brings a new dynamic into the equation because as humans we want to understand everything. This verse says not to rely on your understanding when it comes to finding rest for your soul. Well, the fact is that the yoke principle is one that you will never understand completely.

- *In all your ways acknowledge Him.* In all your ways, this is speaking of your life journey, recognizing Him and His direction.

- *He shall direct your paths.* In other words, He will and is directing your journey toward living the abundant life.

The living-life-abundantly principle is vital for you to find rest for your soul. A soul at rest is one that will eliminate the ugly drama from your life. A soul at rest becomes the eliminator. It will lessen the

A soul at rest becomes the eliminator

anger, agitation, hurt, anxiety, edginess, depression, and any other emotional malady from life journey. You are in a particular stage in your life journey right now. I pray this chapter on rest for your soul will be of value to you no matter what stage you are in.

You may be at the early stage of being in total control of your life and have not experienced this rest for your soul. Maybe you are in the brokenness stage, or possibly you have gone through the cocoon stage and have been transformed. You might be somewhere in the transparency stage where you are approachable to hurting people that don't have rest in their soul. Some reading this chapter have been living the abundant life for a season and understand the yoke principle, leading to their abundant life. I encourage you that no matter what stage you are in to begin applying these principles to your life journey. Keep stretching forth, like a runner in a race, to gain the prize of the high calling of Christ which I believe is living an abundant life.

Probing and Pondering, Chapter Eleven

WRITING YOUR STORY

- Your story line in Chapter 11: "A Restful Soul"

"Instead, you ought to say, 'If the Lord wills,
we shall live and do this or that.'"
—James 4:15

EXPLORE: Study the scriptures to enhance your story line.

- *"God's promise of entering his rest still stands, so we ought to tremble with fear that some of you might fail to experience it."* —Hebrews 4:1, NLT

- *"Come to Me, all you who labor and are heavy laden, and I will give you rest. Take My yoke upon you and learn from Me, for I am gentle and lowly in heart, and you will find rest for your souls. For My yoke is easy and My burden is light."* — Matthew 11:28–30

- *Those who live in the shelter of the Most High will find rest in the shadow of the Almighty. This I declare about the Lord: He alone is my refuge, my place of safety; he is my God, and I trust him.* —Psalm 91:1–2, NLT

- *"This is what the Lord says: 'Stop at the crossroads and look around. Ask for the old, godly way, and walk in it. Travel its path, and you will find rest for your souls.' But you reply, 'No, that's not the road we want!'"* —Jeremiah 6:16, NLT

ENGAGE: developing your story line

- "When you seek rest for your restless soul would you consider finding it inside a yoke?" —Albert Schuessler

    1. Do you ever have moments when it seems your soul is restless, edgy, agitated, and anxious?

    2. Take a moment with your group and discuss your understanding of Ephesians 3:16.

    3. Share as a group how you each came to know Jesus Christ as your personal Savior.

    4. Discuss the dynamics of finding rest for your soul while in the yoke of Christ.

    5. Talk it over as to how spiritual rest could affect your physical rest.

    6. Discuss among you as to what stage you think you are in concerning your life story—brokenness, transformation, transparency, or abundant life.

ENACT: applying to your story line

- "Your transformation in the cocoon is your transportation to the yoke of Jesus Christ." —Albert Schuessler

    1. Take a moment and stop at the crossroads to double check the direction you are headed.

    2. Analyze the inner war you may be experiencing to see if you might be your own enemy.

3. Come up with a plan to exercise your spiritual soul as well as your physical body.

4. Ask yourself as to whether you have crossed the comma in John 10:10 and are experiencing the abundant life.

EMPLOY: living out your story line

- "Yielding to God's direction in your travel is important in finding rest for your soul." —Albert Schuessler

1. Provide a quiet and restful soul to a world culture that is agitated and angry.

2. Let your transparency expose your restful soul to those around you.

3. Allow your restful soul to be an invitation to those who are fighting an inward war of self-destruction.

4. Disciple someone that is experiencing restlessness on how they, too, can yield to the yoke of Jesus and find rest for their soul.

Praying for ownership: Father, my soul has been agitated in the past, and I pray for a restful soul today and in the future. Lord, thank You for directing me to Your yoke. I would never have searched for a restful soul inside a yoke. I am grateful that Your spiritual nutrients flow through Jesus into my life through the Holy Spirit. I want to cast my cares upon You right now, heavenly Father. I know You care for me. Thank You, Jesus, for Your abundant life being lived through me at the present time, providing me with a peaceful soul.

CHAPTER 12

A Peaceful Mind

"You will keep him in perfect peace, whose mind is stayed on You,
Because he trusts in You."
—Isaiah 26:3

"Be anxious for nothing, but in everything by prayer and supplication,
with thanksgiving, let your requests be made known to God;
and the peace of God, which surpasses all understanding, will
guard your hearts and minds through Christ Jesus."
—Philippians 4:6–7

"And let the peace of God rule in your hearts,
to which also you were called in one body; and be thankful."
—Colossians 3:15

"For to be carnally minded is death;
but to be spiritually minded is life and peace."
—Romans 8:6

"Peace of mind will keep you from giving
someone a piece of your mind."
—Albert Schuessler

"The peace of God is a sentinel guarding your mind
from being attacked by Satan's arsenal."
—Albert Schuessler

It seems appropriate as I come to the final chapter of this book to write about having a peaceful mind. I believe brokenness, transformation, and transparency will carry us to the ultimate experience people desire, and that is a peaceful mind. Too often, many of us are in a battle within our minds. A chaotic war scene is raging throughout our minds, with satanic arrows being fired at us day and night. The world culture is a pro at throwing hand grenades at you to frighten you from finding peace in your mind. A land mine is waiting for you to take the next step to blow you up with each step that you take in the right direction.

On the other hand, the mind can be like a peaceful pasture, a wide-open meadow with sheep grazing in the breeze. It can be tranquil like a quiet walk through the woods, listening to the sounds of nature. The mind is a container of things memorized, a tank where ideas are created, a filter where thoughts are weighed out and accepted or rejected, and a reservoir flowing with so many possibilities being considered for the future. I'm listing a couple of important principles that can lead you to a peaceful mind—a mind that is free from the chaotic drama of everyday living and a mind that is not foggy any longer but is crystal clear.

Anxiety Steals Your Peace

Anxiety is defined as the opposite of peace. When we think of anxiety, we think of agitation and conflict within our minds because anxiety creates so much turmoil in our minds since we are focused on the future happenings in our lives. A deeper meaning of anxiety is uneasiness, nervousness, and apprehension due to our anticipation of a future event. It can be defined as a distress upon the mind that steals your peace. The reason anxiety has such a force in our life journey is because it is created within the mind when we are thinking about what might happen in the future. We spend so much time worrying about the events of tomorrow that we do not enjoy the blessings of today. This is such a waste of energy if we stop to think about its consequences.

We should stop and consider this: God warns us about being anxious for tomorrow. He knows what is in the best interest for your life journey. He knows that being stymied by the cloud of doubt for your future will create mayhem in your life. Therefore, He warns us in the following scripture about the importance of life and the futility of worry:

> *Therefore, I say to you, do not worry about your life, what you will eat or what you will drink; nor about your body, what you will put on. Is not life more than food and the body more than clothing? Look at the birds of the air, for they neither sow nor reap nor gather into barns; yet your heavenly Father feeds them. Are you not of more value than they? Which of you by worrying can add one cubit to his stature?*
> (Matthew 6:25–27)

He is not saying that we should not be concerned about life, but He is saying we should not worry about life. In verse 27, He is saying you cannot add one cubit to your stature. He knows your life, and in verse 26, He compares your life to the birds and how He takes care of them, stating how much more He will take care of you. He clearly makes it apparent that you do not need to worry because of

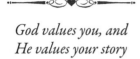

God values you, and He values your story

the value He has placed upon you and your story. God values you, and He values your story.

I appreciate the way James presents the principles of life to us in the following message: *"whereas you do not know what will happen tomorrow. For what is your life? It is even a vapor that appears for a little time and then vanishes away. Instead, you ought to say, "If the Lord wills, we shall live and do this or that"* (James 4:14–15). We do not know what will happen in our lives tomorrow. We might plan for tomorrow and think we know exactly what will happen tomorrow, but God says we do not know what will take place. Tomorrow is a new day, and we might have a new sheet of paper given to us to write our daily journey; but on the other hand, we may have run out of paper and our story ended. It then is pointless for us to worry about tomorrow. To do so will snatch your peace away from you in a flash.

Peace Neutralizes Anxiety

I love the way God is willing and waiting to make the journey with us. He guides us by giving us directions for the path we are to go in our journey. He wants you to experience living an abundant life. He gives you the instruction on how to eliminate the anxiety in your life and to truly experience the peace of mind. *"Be anxious for nothing, but in everything by prayer and supplication, with thanksgiving, let your requests be made known to God; and the peace of God, which surpasses all understanding, will guard your hearts and minds through Christ Jesus"* (Phil. 4:6–7). He begins by telling us not to worry about anything. This seems to be an unreasonable request the apostle Paul is making in this scripture.

It seems that worry is a natural part of human beings. Of course, we should automatically have concern about issues in our lives, but Paul is stating it is not wise to worry about these issues. We should be concerned but not worry about our life situations. God doesn't expect you to handle it; He expects you to hand it over to Him. This statement goes back to Part 1 of this book when I was talking about who is in control of your life. If you are in control of your life then you are going to handle your situation in accordance with the way you think it should be handled.

Now, if you are willing to turn the control of your life over to God, then you will be willing to hand your situation over to Him. When you decide to hand it over to God, you will stop worrying and begin to sense the peace of God filling your mind instead of worry. Notice Paul gives us a very simple formula in these verses we have before us. *First,* He directs our attention to praying to God the Father to overcome our anxiety. I know by experience when going through my pain that prayer was probably the last place I wanted to go. I'm not quite sure why we hesitate to pray. Maybe prayer seems so impersonal, talking to someone we cannot see or touch. Notice in the following scripture God says don't hesitate to pray but come boldly with your request. *"Let us therefore come boldly to the throne of grace, that we may obtain mercy and find grace to help in time of need" (Heb. 4:16).* God reveals His heart of grace to us by saying, "Come boldly and let me help you with your special need today." Please take time while reading this scripture to ponder in your mind the significance of this verse for your life. *Secondly;,* he adds the word *supplication* alongside the word prayer. Obviously prayer and supplication do not have the same definition. It is important to distinguish the difference between the two words if we are going to have peace of mind. Supplication is from the Latin word *supplicare*, which means to humbly plead your case before God.

The root word for supplication is "supple," which is defined as something pliable, soft, flexible, and impressionable. Supplication in the context of prayer, then, would be coming boldly to God with a heart and mind that is pliable, flexible, and impressionable before God. You are asking God to make your heart supple and willing to be bent toward His will and not your will in answering your prayer. He then can mold your mind, spirit, and soul into changing your thoughts and emotions from worry to peace concerning your situational need. *Thirdly,* Paul adds another layer in overcoming our anxious moments in life. I believe using these three words—prayer, supplication, and thanksgiving—is an indication of how difficult it is to rid your minds of worry. Praying with thanksgiving is now added to the equation of having your worries released and emptied from your mind. It certainly is not done by the snap of the finger. You may wonder why we should pray with thanksgiving even though our prayer has not yet been answered. I believe if you pray with boldness and your mind is pliable to the way God will answer your prayer, then you can be grateful for His answer no matter how He answers. It may not be the way you think your prayer should be answered, but you are satisfied it is the way He wanted your prayer to be answered. *Fourthly,* he tells us to let our request be made known to God. In other words, he is saying, "Hand your anxiety over to God and let Him handle it." It is as simple as just telling God what you need for your life, what is troubling you, and the struggle you are facing with your pain. If you want peace of mind that comes along with living the abundant life, then you will have to trust God with the fact that He knows what is best for you.

> *Hand your anxiety over to God and let Him handle it*

A Peace Guards Your Mind

As you journey through your life story, there will be many times that you will have things happening to you that will cause you to worry. Most of the time, they would be defined as some things you are concerned about and not necessarily worried about. However, the issue that brought about your brokenness in your journey was probably painful enough to cause you to worry about what was taking place in your life at that moment. If you have not undergone brokenness in your life at this point, keep in mind that someday you are probably going to suffer in some way. What happens is that worry is like a wall between your heart and mind that will block peace from entering your mind. God has given us the weapon that will destroy that wall which, in turn, will open a passageway for peace to enter mind. The weapon to destroy the blockage is to hand your circumstance over to God in prayer and supplication with thanksgiving.

The promise in the following verse is so profound that it is beyond your reasoning to understand God's peace given to you: *"and the peace of God, which surpasses all understanding, will guard your hearts and minds through Christ Jesus"* (Phil. 4:7). Notice in this verse the apostle Paul is not talking about making peace with God. That peace was made for us by Jesus Christ when He died upon the cross for our sins and by exercising our faith in the finished work of Jesus upon the cross. Here the apostle Paul is speaking simply about the peace of God. It would be futile for me to define this peace since it surpasses all understanding. Though I am not capable of defining this peace, I can express through my experience that it was the catalyst to my living the abundant Christian life. The Greek word for peace in this verse is *eirene* which means to bring together that which is broken or divided. It speaks of bringing together a oneness that is broken and divided. Another way of defining this peace is saying I have it all together. It makes sense when you think about the division between worry and peace.

First, worry is a mind focused on self, and peace is a mind focused on God. *Secondly,* worry focuses on earthly things, and peace focuses on heavenly things. *Thirdly,* worry is centered on self; peace is centered on God. *Fourthly,* worry is the result of fear, and peace is the result of faith. You see this division between the two is what causes the conflict in our life. God's peace settles the conflict, His peace wins the battle, the two divided come together in one, and now peace has won the battle in your mind. The picture unfolds in the following way, in a painful circumstance where your mind is divided between worry and faith. This scenario is very painful and agonizing for anyone. There is no way to live an abundant life with your mind divided between worry and faith. Since God's desire is for us to live an abundant life, He provides protection for us to move forward in our life journey with a peaceful mind. What is so amazing about this protection He provides for the future is that He provides it with the same peace He has given to you. His peace is so powerful that it becomes a sentinel to guard your heart and mind through Christ Jesus. Guarding your heart is paramount in your living an abundant life in your future journey.

Guard Your Heart to Find Peace

The following verse promises you perfect peace if your mind is fixed on God: *"You will keep him in perfect peace, whose mind is stayed on You, Because he trusts in You"* (Isa. 26:3). Living an abundant life is the destination we have been aiming for in our journey throughout this book. I believe the abundant life is defined as a joyful heart, a restful soul, and a peaceful mind. Notice the message of the verse is having your mind focused on God. In other words, it means He is in control when your mind is fixed on Him. Part of brokenness is to get our minds off who you are and to fix your mind on who He is. Our brokenness and transformation exercise our faith to the point we stop leaning on our own understanding and lean on God. God's peace is called perfect peace, which means it is without fault or defect and is complete. The promise is that He will keep or guard your mind as a sentry guards a fortress.

The biblical secret to a peaceful mind is to fix your mind on God almighty and trust Him for the outcome of your life journey. With your mind fixed on God, allowing Him to be in control of your life journey, will yield great dividends for your journey. It produces genuine peace that can govern your heart according to the following scripture: *"And let the peace of God rule in your hearts, to which also you were called in one body; and be thankful"* (Col. 3:15).

We sometimes don't realize how important it is to understand the power of the heart working in our everyday life. The meaning of the word *heart* being used in the context of this book is speaking of our inner being defined as our spirit, soul, mind, and heart. You must pay attention to this part of your life to experience an abundant life. It is such an important factor in forming your story and later for you to own your story. It is so easy for us to focus on the things about us that are visible in relation to our bodies. We are concerned about how we look, our weight, our hair style, our nails, our teeth, our physique, our age, our wrinkles, our muscle loss, and our facial look. It is natural to be concerned about the physical part of us, that part we can literally see.

However, God makes it clear that we are to be more concerned about the invisible and spiritual part of who we are. Notice the admonishment in the following verse about guarding your heart: *"Guard your heart above all else, for it determines the course of your life"*

(Prov. 4:23, NLT). God is very pointed in this verse—above everything else that you are concerned about in life, guard your heart. Your heart is the number one factor that you are to be focused on. He then gives us the reason why it is the number one factor. Your heart determines the course of your journey. Everything you say and do comes from the heart. When you go back in time, recalling the timeline of your life, I think you will find that the condition of your inner person has been the most important influence in your life journey. A guarded heart and a mind fixed on God produces the peace found in an abundant life.

The Three Chords of Abundant Life

The book of Ecclesiastes speaks of the strength of a three-strand cord: *"Though one may be overpowered by another, two can withstand him. And a threefold cord is not quickly broken."* (Eccl. 4:12) I believe the three subjects we have focused on in Part 4 of this book are significant to entering an abundant Christian life. The three chapter titles of Part 4 are having a joyful heart, a restful soul, and a peaceful mind. The heart, soul, and mind cover three important aspects of the human being. They are difficult for us to understand and to keep in check because they are invisible to us, and yet they are such powerful forces within our emotional life. Our brokenness and transformation will lead us to an abundant life if we understand the process and know that it is all taking place in our inner being. However, if we become *bitter* during our brokenness, we will continue in our journey days, weeks, months, and sometimes years in our emotional pain. We will use this pain, claiming it to be our identity into the future, and we will never come to the place of feeling comfortable owning our story. If we become *better* in our brokenness, then the worry and pain will be exchanged for the peace of God in our life.

In this case, our identity will be found the Lord Jesus Christ. We choose pain or gain for our identity. Not only do we have the three chords of our inner life—the heart, soul, and mind—there are also three significant

We choose pain or gain for our identity

words that we desire to fill our inner life. They are fruit that we can never produce in our heart, soul, and mind. We cannot work for them, we cannot buy them, and we cannot produce them. Only God can empower our inner person with them. We long for joy, rest, and peace to counteract sadness, turmoil, and conflict in our lives. These three words are the cream that rises to the top of our lives.

It is my prayer that these three spiritual principles have or will help you to get past the comma in John 10:10. Experiencing joy, rest, and peace will move you across the threshold from life, to living an abundant life. I believe that the journey is worth living in spite of whatever you have experienced, as long as it carries you across the comma to an abundant life.

Thank God or Make a Choice

I am sure some of you reading this book have experienced most of the things I have presented, and you now are living an abundant life. Everyone's journey is different and takes a different road, but nevertheless you have arrived at the destination of an abundant life. If this is you, I encourage you to thank God for His love and grace given to you and choose to continue your present journey. Some of you may be right in the middle of your brokenness today and are working through your pain. Maybe you are in your messy cocoon and dying to self at this very moment. I encourage you to follow the plan in this book and allow God to be in control of your life so that you will eventually experience peace of mind and an abundant life.

OWN YOUR STORY BEFORE YOUR STORY OWNS YOU

You will need to make some unpleasant choices in the future, but they will be worth your decision. Then there may be some reading this book, who have never experienced any unpleasant circumstances in your life up to this point. I encourage you to keep the principles of this book in your mind in case someday a situation will blindside you and create chaos in your life. At that time, you will need to make a choice to choose better over bitter. Above all, when the time comes in any of the scenarios presented in this book, consider owning your story before your story owns you. God bless your journey! Your story, name it and claim it!

Your story, name it and claim it!

200

Probing and Pondering, Chapter Twelve

WRITING YOUR STORY

- Your story line in Chapter 12: "A Peaceful Mind"

> *"Instead, you ought to say, 'If the Lord wills,*
> *we shall live and do this or that.'"*
> —James 4:15

EXPLORE: Study the scriptures to enhance your story line.

- *"You will keep him in perfect peace, whose mind is stayed on You, because he trusts in You."* —Isaiah 26:3

- *"Be anxious for nothing, but in everything by prayer and supplication, with thanksgiving, let your requests be made known to God; and the peace of God, which surpasses all understanding, will guard your hearts and minds through Christ Jesus."* —Philippians 4:6–7

- *"And let the peace of God rule in your hearts, to which also you were called in one body; and be thankful."* —Colossians 3:15

- *"For to be carnally minded is death; but to be spiritually minded is life and peace."* —Romans 8:6

ENGAGE: developing your story line

- "Peace of mind will keep you from giving someone a piece of your mind." —Albert Schuessler

    1. Do you have a history of living in a chaotic drama environment during your informative years of life?

2. Share with others as to the day-to-day level of anxiety you encounter.

3. Discuss what it means to you when Philippians 4:6–7 states, "Hand your problem over to God."

4. *Eirene*, the Greek word for peace, means bringing back together that which has been broken. Such as a relationship. Ponder that thought in your mind.

5. Discuss with others as to how peace has the power to be a sentinel guarding your mind.

6. Just for fun, have your group come up with your definition of peace. Keep in mind, it is a peace beyond understanding.

ENACT: applying to your story line

- "The peace of God is a sentinel guarding your mind from being attacked by Satan's arsenal." —Albert Schuessler

1. What are some ways you can make sure you are guarding your heart diligently?

2. Develop a plan for the Holy Spirit to strengthen your inner person.

3. Add to your prayer a time to be pliable through supplication and thanksgiving.

4. Develop a lifestyle of peace in order to live an abundant life.

EMPLOY: living out your story line

- *"Guard your heart above all else, for it determines the course of your life."* —Proverbs 4:23, NLT

  1. Allow people to see your peace through your words and actions played out before them.

  2. Share with others your life journey on how you are experiencing an abundant life.

  3. Impact the life of others with your three chords of the abundant life, consisting of joy, rest, and peace.

  4. Never underestimate the power of your peace to influence those who live in chaos.

Praying for ownership: Father, I thank You for the peace of God that passeth all understanding. Lord, I want to handle the problems of my life by myself. I pray that You will teach me and encourage me to hand them over to You. Father, my mind is powerful and can create images for the future that stimulates worry and anxiety in my life. I pray for the joy, rest, and peace that only You can provide for me. My desire and passion is to live an abundant life. I need Your strength to carry out my desire for such a life.

Conclusion

"Own it" is a catchphrase that you have heard many times. It means taking responsibility for what a person has said or done. I am defining this phrase as a person owning the outcome of a decision that they have made concerning their life journey. Own your story before your story owns you. Ownership has a sense of pride and dignity, along with pleasure and satisfaction. You may never share certain events that have happened in your story, and that's all right. The main thing is to make sure you own that event. Then if you feel free to share the event, by all means do share.

When building interstate highways across America from the East Coast to the West Coast, the engineers faced many challenges in the designing and construction of the highway. The challenges included valleys, mountains, curves, rivers, forest, desert, rock, and sand in consideration of their engineering plans to complete the highway.

In your life journey, "Own your story before your story owns you," you have learned throughout this book that there are many challenges you must face to complete your journey. There are valleys, mountains, rivers, curves, walls, and dead ends that you will need to trek through in order to complete your journey. These are all a part of building your life story. Some of these obstacles may seem insurmountable to you at the present time. My prayer is, as you process the contents of this book, you will *see beyond what you see* and will continue in your game of life until you reach your goal of an abundant life. There are so many questions to life, and I have added many answers to those questions in this book. My life journey has provided me with the answers, and I have shared them with you in the four main parts of this book.

A great deal of time was spent in working our way through the misunderstood subject of *brokenness*. Brokenness is all about the control of life. The reason we are reluctant to give in to brokenness is because we do not want to give up the control of our lives. Control means turning loose of the helm of our lives and allowing God to steer our life in the right direction.

In Part 2, we have a microscopic view of nature's awesome process of metamorphosis. In this section we were able to mentally visualize how we can apply this principle to our spiritual lives. The microscope revealed to us the messy inner workings of the cocoon. In the cocoon, the caterpillar's cells begin to die with a few minimal cells surviving and eventually forming the butterfly inside the cocoon. We learned that the butterfly coming out of the cocoon had the same DNA as the caterpillar going into the cocoon. In spiritual life, it pictures how messy it gets in our cocoon as we are dying to self and coming forth as a new person represented by the beautiful butterfly.

In Part 3, we moved over to the completed side of our brokenness and transformation. Here we find our lives open up and become exposed through our *transparency*. We discovered that brokenness and transformation changes our lives in so many ways. Transparency certainly deals with our pride, bringing us to a state of humility. In a negative sense, transparency causes us to become very vulnerable and often criticized by our friends. However, in a positive way, it allows us to be approachable by welcoming other people into our lives. You will become a breath of fresh air to those who are experiencing the pain of brokenness and transformation in their lives.

Part 4 is like a spiritual victory lap celebrating the most sought-after position in life. You finally crossed the finish line, took the checkered flag, and received the trophy for pressing forward to the goal in life that so many people are searching for and yet, so few ever find. That goal or prize is the high calling of God in Christ Jesus (Phil. 3:14). What will that prize consist of and look like to you? To visualize what it must look like, imagine yourself climbing Mt. Everest, and you finally reached the highest pinnacle of the mountain. What do you see? You would see one of the most beautiful and majestic sights you could ever lay your eyes upon. In our spiritual life, it would be like standing on top of Mt. Everest and looking around, and this is what you would see: the beauty of a joyful heart, a restful soul, and a peaceful mind. The Bible calls it an abundant life.

It has been the dream of my life to write this book and to share with you the great joy of life. To share with you the importance of Adam's story, the very first story ever told, and to share with you the importance of your story being written at the present time. Many stories have been written between Adam's story and your story but none any more important than yours. Thanks for reading the book and allowing me the honor of sharing your story with you.

Remember, one bad chapter doesn't mean the story is over. Failing is not a disgrace unless you make it the last chapter of your book. Own your story before your story owns you.

About the Author

 Albert Schuessler was born and raised on a farm in rural Kansas. Albert became a believer in Christ as a young boy while his family attended a small Baptist Church near their home. His faith was the catalyst in forming his own story to where his journey is today. He attended and graduated from High School in Valley Center, Kansas. He is an artist and enjoys oil painting. He is an author who has written a book titled "The Holy Potholes of Christianity." Albert is a graduate of Baptist Bible College in Springfield, Missouri. After graduating from Bible college, he entered the pastorate and has been pastoring for 53 years serving Faith Bible Baptist Church in Valley Center, Kansas for 28 years. He has been married to his wife Shirley for 63 years. They have three sons, ten grandchildren and 14 great grandchildren.

CPSIA information can be obtained
at www.ICGtesting.com
Printed in the USA
JSHW021557220622
27298JS00004BA/20